230.4
H38f

64091

FORGIVENESS and HOPE

FORGIVENESS

and HOPE

TOWARD A THEOLOGY FOR
PROTESTANT CHRISTIAN EDUCATION

by Rachel Henderlite

JOHN KNOX PRESS, Richmond, Virginia

Library of Congress Catalogue Card Number: 61-13518

Third printing 1963

To all lay men and women
who are giving themselves
to the educational work of the church

Preface

The chapters which follow here were originally prepared and delivered on the invitation of the faculty and students of Louisville Theological Seminary as the George McNutt Lectures for 1959. As such they dealt with the very practical issue of the church's own program of life and work and the grave importance of reflecting therein the church's historic faith.

The invitation to present these lectures marked a high moment in my life, as did the whole experience of preparing and delivering them. There never was a more gracious body of persons than these professors and students, their wives and families and friends, and never an association more thoroughly enjoyed. Their willingness to hear a woman to the end was a tribute to their own genuineness rather than to the stuff of the lectures. Their courtesy and warmth throughout the week was an experience not to be forgotten.

The subject of the lectures is one of great concern to me and has been for a number of years. For the most part I have dealt with this subject in the past, as here, in relation to the educational work of the church, although the lectures were originally put in the broader frame of the total work of the church; and revisions in the lectures have been made with this particular interest in education in mind. It has seemed to me no less than tragic that so much of what passes for Christian education as I have known it has been informed by the philosophy of secular America as much as by the gospel of Jesus Christ and that Christian education has been distorted by the improper coalition. I have followed with the keenest appreciation, therefore, the succession of books dealing with this problem that have appeared in recent years: Shelton Smith's *Faith and Nurture*, which served to lift up the problem for many people; James D. Smart's *The Teaching Ministry of the Church*, which directly attacked the sub-Christian aspects of the church's approach to education; the books by Randolph Crump Miller, which have called attention to new possibilities opened up

7

for us by biblical theology; the writings of D. Campbell Wyckoff; the recent book by Iris V. Cully on *The Dynamics of Christian Education.* All of these and others have, it seems to me, moved us farther toward the possibilities of a solid structure of Christian education based on the theology of the Christian church. Each of them has approached the problem from a particular perspective —some of them largely critical of the past efforts in Christian education, others proposing directions in which the church may and should now move.

My own effort here duplicates none of these and takes issue with none, although there are points of difference. These chapters attempt to lift up for study some elements of Protestant theology that have been neglected in the practical work of the church, although not necessarily in its preaching, and to indicate some of the effects that would be felt in education if due attention were given to these elements. No claim is made for comprehensiveness. The job of working out an adequate and comprehensive theology for Christian education lies in the future.

These chapters propose the doctrine of justification by faith as an appropriate organizing principle for such a theology and lift up four problems for consideration: the meaning of faith, the nature of man, the nature of new life, and the meaning of history. In other words, these chapters deal with epistemology, anthropology, ethics, and eschatalogy. They do not so much seek to define the doctrines with precision as to indicate the measure of responsibility and the nature of the responsibility entrusted to the church in these regards. It is the hope of the writer that these chapters will serve the church in two ways: (1) that they will push more competent theologians into the task I have begun here, for the church is in dire need of having the job done adequately; and (2) that they will, even in this tentative form, open the eyes of teachers and parents, and laymen generally, to the supreme importance of the work of Christian education and to the utter necessity that it reflect in the content it teaches, in the procedures it follows, and in the spirit that pervades it, the gospel of God's grace.

It is no ordinary task to which Christ calls the church. The task of Christian education is the task of the whole church—that of bringing men and women and boys and girls continually into the presence of God so that they may open their hearts to him and be taken hold of by his transforming power. No other task than this has been given to the church.

If these chapters can serve in any way to assist the church in understanding and carrying out this task, I shall be gratified.

RACHEL HENDERLITE.

RICHMOND, VIRGINIA

Contents

FORGIVENESS and HOPE

"That you may know what is the hope to which he has called you, what are the riches of his glorious inheritance in the saints." (Ephesians 1:18)

The Need for a Theology of Protestant Christian Education

THE SITUATION CALLING FOR THIS STUDY

Creativity and Paradox

The mid-twentieth century is a period of singular creativity in Christian education in the Protestant churches in America. Evidences of this can be seen on every hand and interpretations of it vary as widely as its manifestations. The deepening of theological insight occasioned no doubt by the distress of wars on a global scale, the development of biblical theology with its rediscovery of the Bible as a book with a message of hope for the world, the declining faith of educators in the power of human freedom and their increased respect for the heritage of the past, the discovery on the part of psychologists of the deep mysteries of human nature, the growing awareness of the significance of social relationships in the development of personality, the emerging concepts of the church, the increasing interest in the laity—these and many other factors at work in our day come together to make this what some believe to be one of the great creative periods in the educational work of the church, possibly the most creative period we have known.

When we speak of the creativity of this period, we must speak also and at once of the paradoxes and confusions that mark the work of the church today. Paradoxes and confusion always accompany creativity, and the direction of the creative movement is not always clear. For instance, at the very time when great denominational branches of the church are becoming aware of their oneness with other denominational branches of the church as the living body of Christ, these same denominations are seeking the peculiar marks that set them apart from one another. The ecumenical movement, which has arisen as a dominant movement in church life in this century, has made and is making the great Protestant denominations aware of their basic similarities; but it is at the same time requiring each denomination to make a closer scrutiny of its own distinctive beliefs and practices and of the peculiar contribution it has to make to the Protestant church as a whole. And the ecumenical movement is not weaker because of this two-way movement, but stronger.

Moreover, in its concern to carry out its distinctive task in the twentieth century more adequately, the church is looking to institutions and disciplines outside the church for technical assistance of many kinds—for ways of understanding human development and interpersonal relationships, for the meaning of communication and for technical skills in the modern methods of communication, for skills in personal counseling, for educational theory and practice. Thus, for example, a mission hospital draws on the science of medicine for the knowledge it requires to perform its task. The church knows itself to be a part of the world and to be dependent on the world, at the same time that the church is called out of the world to serve the world. The relationship of church to world is such that the church must make use of the world's skills and knowledge if it is to meet the world's need, but the church must not allow the world to temper its message or to modify its task. Consequently the church's very reliance on the world requires the church to dig deeper into its own faith, seeking the distinctive aspects of the church's life and work which set it apart as church from all other institutions in the world.

The Threats to the Church

Two dangers have threatened the church in recent years, however, and continue to threaten it in this period of creativity—dangers that find their source in these two paradoxes just described. The first is the danger inherent in all co-operative endeavor, that in the zeal to overcome their differences and realize the oneness of the church, the churches may pay too dear a price and purchase a too thin uniformity rather than a rich ecumenicity. The second is the danger always facing the church, that in relying on the world for the scientific data and technical skills that can come to the church only from the world, the church will at the same time appropriate uncritically into its theology the presuppositions about the nature of the universe which frequently characterize a scientific or technical era. Let us look at each of these perils of the church in turn.

The first danger to which reference has been made is the danger that in their eagerness to realize the oneness of the church of Jesus Christ and work together at the gigantic tasks that confront all the churches equally, the churches will be betrayed into surrendering some of the distinctive traits that mark them as the church. It is interesting that in the early stages of the ecumenical movement this danger became apparent to many denominational branches of the church to such degree that a countermovement began, in which the strength of ecumenical organizations and faith and order studies have been matched by strong alliances of churches along denominational lines.

The same sort of countermovement may be seen in the educational work of the American Protestant churches. Because Christian education is the primary concern of these chapters, it will be necessary to spend some time in analysis of this situation.

Within American Protestantism around the turn of the century, when the need for a strong curriculum of religious education became apparent, the gigantic nature of the task made co-operation among the major denominations seem a wise and necessary procedure. As far back as 1824 there had been an American Sunday

School Union, which for many years pioneered in establishing Sunday schools and preparing materials. In 1873 the International Uniform Lessons were begun. In 1922 through the merging of two co-operative organizations, the International Sunday School Association and the Sunday School Council of the Evangelical Denominations, the International Council of Religious Education was founded, an organization now serving as the Division of Christian Education of the National Council of the Churches of Christ in the United States of America.

The task of this organization, to service the constituent churches in the area of Christian education, has been a mammoth one, undertaken with vision and courage. The fruits of its labors are many and varied. Most Protestants in America have profited by its work far more richly than they know. What follows here is no attempt to be critical of the National Council of Churches or of the Division of Christian Education, for the contribution to the Protestant church life of this organization and of this division has been incalculable. What follows is an attempt to point out one aspect of the course that curriculum development has taken in America—not to censure, and certainly not to fix the blame. The fact that recovery from the malady can occur and is occurring under the aegis of the National Council of Churches, as the disease did, is a noteworthy fact, and gives evidence of remarkable resiliency and integrity on the part of the National Council of Churches and its constituent denominations.

In attempting to work together to produce the basis of a curriculum of Christian education that would be usable in many different denominations, it was inevitable that the denominations should surrender certain distinctive denominational emphases and that only the broad aspects of the Christian faith common to all major branches of Protestantism should be included in the common literature of curriculum. It is true, however, that safeguards of many kinds were built into the process of curriculum construction in order to permit revision and re-enrichment of educational materials by the denominations, and as a result the churches have on the whole been satisfied with the product.

This elimination of particular denominational emphasis and the concentration on the common core of the Christian faith can work toward a far stronger treatment of the Christian faith, for theology is always strongest when it emphasizes the central convictions of the church upon which all Christians agree rather than the peripheral matters on which denominations have differed—and to a large degree it may be said that it has done so. Had there not been other factors at work also, this might have proved to be no problem. But the thin uniformity which always threatens ecumenicity was already coupled with a liberal theology that moved toward humanism, and this was aggravated no doubt by the influence of secular forces in society. Particularly was this aggravated by the uncritical acceptance in education of humanistic philosophies which prevail widely in American public education. To this aspect of the problem we shall now turn.

The second danger to which reference has been made is the danger that in turning to other disciplines and other institutions for information and technical skills as it seeks to chart its way in education, the church may allow itself to be betrayed into relying on the presuppositions on which these disciplines and institutions rest rather than on the presuppositions of the Christian faith. The weakness of Christian education in recent years has been just this—that in going to secular education and other foundation disciplines like psychology and sociology for assistance, the church has allowed itself to be tragically influenced, even invaded, by their secular philosophies. So subtle has been this invasion, indeed, that the church has in recent years moved back and forth between Christian faith and pragmatism or humanism without actually being aware of its inconsistency.

How this came about can be quickly told. About the turn of the century and later, persons within the church began to feel that Christian education was falling short of meeting the needs of men and women and boys and girls for a living faith. As a result the church began to draw on psychology and general education for ways of teaching that would take into account the differences in people and the need for a contemporary message that speaks immediately to life. This strengthened greatly the methods of teaching being used in the church and contributed to the beginning of a strong religious education movement in Protestantism. But without any intention on the part of religious educators it led a large part of the Protestant church away from its conviction that the gospel is the starting point of the church's work to what we know as person-centered religious education.

In these fifty years one great stream of Protestant Christian education, because it has been person-centered or experienced-centered, shaping its curriculum upon the needs of the person rather than upon the gospel, has adopted a number of principles and practices which have doubtful kinship to the Christian faith. One such practice has been that of using the Bible primarily for helping to meet immediate and specific human needs rather than for understanding what God has done. In thus using the Bible the church has obviously misused the Bible and lost the real meaning of the gospel, as may be seen in the spiritual illiteracy of many of our church members today. Another such doubtful practice is related to statements of the goals of religious education. Relying uncritically on psychology, the church has often stated its basic educational goal in such phrases as "to bring man to maturity," or "to bring man to the fullest realization of himself"—a goal which reflects the philosophical position we call "idealistic perfectionism" but which must be recognized as at least secondary to, if not in actual disharmony with, the aspiration of the Christian faith.

Such expressions of the goal of Christian education are at variance with the Christian faith at two crucial points: (1) In speaking of bringing man to maturity one is likely to overlook man's basic need for a complete conversion from an old way to a new way of life in Christ, a conversion which cannot be described simply in terms of growth toward maturity. (2) This statement of goals seems to rest naïvely on the assumption that man is capable of bringing himself or another to such maturity or fulfillment, overlooking the biblical truth that any change that takes place in man's essential being is the work of God in Jesus Christ.

Such uncritical acceptance of humanistic ways of thought leads inevitably to a twofold idolatry, in which man is seen as the end toward which the church works, and as the power which activates the process. The root of sin is the assumption that man is himself the beginning and end of all endeavor, and that man can bring about change in himself or in another man. This is the denial of God and the refusal of creaturehood.

A Resurgence of Faith

In this creative period we face today, theologians are beginning to point out the idolatry of such a beginning point and goal—and the danger to the church of working within such a frame of reference—and they are beginning to call us back to the Christian faith. Aware of the danger of being led away from our central convictions, many of the major Protestant denominations have in the past decade been driven to make thorough appraisals of their educational work and to develop new programs of education with emphases that reflect their distinctive interpretations of the Christian faith. The Presbyterian Church, USA, was the first major denomination to express dissatisfaction with current patterns of education by withdrawing from the co-operative processes of curriculum development to create a new "Faith and Life" curriculum, stressing the proclamation of the Word of God as the organizing principle of the curriculum of the church. The Protestant Episcopal Church soon thereafter began their development of a curriculum known as the Seabury Series—a curriculum which is organized on the principle that the gospel is Good News which meets man today at the point of his greatest need. Other great churches have felt the necessity for the same kind of study of their educational work, each one seeking to develop a curriculum that represents the real meaning of the Christian faith as this church understands it, and that will serve to communicate the Christian faith to man in the twentieth century.

What will be the outcome of this period of creativity in Protestant Christian education it is too soon to tell. Whether the churches will, for instance, do less of their educational work co-operatively, or whether the co-operation will be of a different sort and take place at a different level, is not clear. But the emergence of deep theological concern for the developments in education on the part of the church is reassuring. The jealousy of the churches for the right to define educational principles and to construct educational programs in harmony with their own basic convictions—a jealousy which reflects the church's rightful claim on Christian education as an expression of church life—suggests that Christian education may be in for a period of solid and creative advance.

The Need for Careful Study

If such a period of advance is to be our fortune, however, it will be achieved only by the most careful and exacting work on the part of the churches. A program of education that reflects the essence of a society is hard won. Particularly is this true when the society in question is the church, which looks at life in one way, set down in the world, which looks at life in a completely different way. The influence of world upon church is very great, and the temptation to the church to compromise with the world is almost irresistible. The difficulty is that when the church surrenders its distinctive convictions about God and man, or allows these to be modified in the direction of the secular and the worldly, the church no longer has an educational function to perform.

The matter to be explored in these chapters concerns the problem which all Protestant churches in America are facing in one way or another, and which must be faced squarely if Christian education is to advance solidly, as seems now to be possible. This is a problem which may be expressed in terms of Christian education, although it actually concerns the entire life and work of the church. Has not the church in allying itself with secular education and adopting some of its presuppositions been betrayed into denying some of the central affirmations of the Christian faith? Is it not necessary to build the educational work of the church upon the church's own affirmations of faith even at the risk of conflicting at points with the foundation disciplines like the man sciences upon which education is thought to rely?

Perhaps the word "education" itself is proving inadequate for describing the process of communicating the Christian faith from one generation to another. Is it not possible that when the church speaks of Christian education it has reference to a particular kind of communication that gets its distinctive character from the Christian faith and that may not be precisely "education" at all? If so, can we develop a theology for Christian education that will safeguard the character of Christian education as a distinctive discipline by which the Christian faith may be appropriately communicated from one generation to another?

As one looks at the educational work of the Protestant churches throughout the country, four tendencies appear which indicate the profound necessity for rooting Christian education more deeply in the gospel, indeed, for clarifying the implications of Protestant theology for Protestant Christian education. An analysis of these tendencies in the light of the Christian faith may enable the churches to build more solidly in this creative period.

1. The tendency to teach about God as though he were the object of intellectual inquiry only.

2. The tendency to deal with people as though we could mold them into whatever pattern we wish, as though we were God to create man in our own image.

3. The tendency to teach moral axioms as though man could become good by merely deciding to do so.

4. The tendency to picture the Kingdom of God statically and propositionally and to preserve the church as an institution as though God were doing nothing and going nowhere.

Such tendencies are not peculiar to the church today. In every age some such defections from the faith are apparent in the life of the church. They reflect the perennial attempt of the church to escape God's judgment and his offer of regeneration and new life, and to offer its people some mild form of faith which is not likely to get out of hand.

In every generation the church has tried to control the gospel rather than be controlled by it. Our generation is no exception. The fact that this has been characteristic of every generation is no reason for complacency, however. It is important to recognize that such tendencies as these are in basic disharmony with the Christian faith as it has been made known to us in the New Testament and reaffirmed in the Protestant Reformation, and that they require of us that we examine afresh the central affirmations of our faith for the light they will throw upon the educational program of the church.

Our task then is this: Can we lift up the distinctive emphasis of Protestant theology and use it as a guide so that the church's life and work and its basic convictions may be all of a piece? Can we discover the characteristics that would mark the educational work of the church if this were based precisely on the theology of the Protestant Reformation, which the churches in fact hold as their creedal base? In a recent celebration of Reformation Day in Kansas City, President Emeritus John A. Mackay of Princeton Theological Seminary said: "What is needed today is not the rediscovery of forgotten truths, but the restoration of accepted truths to their rightful place in the thought and life of the church."

THE PROBLEM: THE WORK OF THE CHURCH BASED ON JUSTIFICATION BY FAITH

In an attempt to take hold of the problem now facing the church, that of articulating a theology of Christian education which grows out of the biblical faith, there is no better starting place than the doctrine of justification by faith, which has been a key doctrine in Protestant theology since its beginning.

Reasons for the Choice of Topic

It is not necessary, one may assume, to justify the use of the doctrine of justification by faith as the starting point for a theology for Protestant Christian education. The work of any institution to strengthen its own life and to carry out its mission must rest on presuppositions that lie at its very heart. When any society seeks to propagate itself, it must establish its message and program on its own distinctive character, on those features of its life that mark its difference from other societies. This, for churches of the Reformed faith, will be found in this doctrine which serves as the organizing principle of much of the Protestant theology, and in the aspects of its life which may be defined by this doctrine. In this doctrine will be found the basic truths of the Christian faith which, if rightly understood and taken seriously, should serve as the organizing principle of a profound theology of Christian education true to the nature of the Christian faith and fit to serve the needs of modern man.

It was the static view of righteousness characteristic of Roman Catholic thought at its lowest period that was the occasion for the Reformation in the fifteenth and sixteenth centuries. Obedience to the law was seen as God's requirement for man, and little stress was placed on the reality of dynamic personal faith on the part of the common man. About this conception of righteousness had grown up a whole body of casuistry and an inflexible system of rewards and punishments. The revolt of Martin Luther against the Church of Rome was a revolt against this system, because Martin Luther's own travail of soul had led him to a belief in God's active love which goes out seeking man no matter what.

When Martin Luther emerged from his struggle with the formalism and legalism and consequent corruption of the Roman Church, he held in his hand and in his heart the doctrine of justification by faith, which lay at the center of Paul's gospel and which is the central message of the Bible about God's dealing with men—that God loves man with an unconditional love and that he spends himself to reclaim him, bringing him into his family if man will let him do so—if man has faith. "When I grasped that," says Luther, "I felt myself to be reborn and to have gone through open doors into paradise. The whole of scripture took on a new meaning."

The task of attempting to formulate a theology for Protestant Christian education is a difficult one. The idea of justification by faith, says Paul Tillich, "is strange to the man of today, and even to Protestant people in the churches; indeed, as I have over and over again the opportunity to learn, it is so strange to modern man that there is scarcely any way of making it intelligible to him." It is, says Emil Brunner, "the great inversion of existence." And it will have to be an inversion of a great deal of the thinking of Christian educators. For much that we have done has fallen short of the gospel and has resulted in our bringing up a generation of fine, decent Americans who have no real grasp of the difference between natural morality and life under the Lordship of Christ.

The Point of View

The adoption of this phrase "justification by faith" as the center of these considerations does not mean that we shall see it as our function to go back to the theology of the sixteenth century. We shall return to the Bible as Luther and Calvin did, seeking for a biblical faith in Jesus Christ, but we shall return to the Bible as the twentieth-century men and women we are, not as first-century or sixteenth-century men and women. If in so doing we are led to use words and phrases the Reformers found suggestive, it will be with the intent of using them with the fullness of meaning they have for us today, rather than slavishly seeking the meaning put into them by others. Thus, although we shall refer to Calvin and Luther, we shall take neither the words of these men nor the words of the Westminister Confession of Faith as authority; but rather we shall follow the principle so important to Calvin and Luther and the writers of the Westminster Confession—namely, looking for the truth of the gospel as contained in the Scriptures and as interpreted for the church by the Holy Spirit.

Justification by faith is not suggested here as a single doctrine of Reformed theology standing by itself. It is used as a key phrase of a whole system of theology. It takes into account a grace extended to man freely and unconditionally, which when received and entered into is itself the transforming and sanctifying power of the new life in Christ. It takes into account the dynamic nature of faith as a man's total surrender of himself in response to God's grace.

It shall be the purpose of these chapters to explore the meaning of this central doctrine of biblical and Reformation thought for its bearing on some of the problems of Christian education now facing the church. Four great emphases of Protestant theology will be dealt with, emphases which grow out of the doctrine of justification by faith and which bear directly on the four tendencies in church life referred to above.

Chapter one, "Words Without Knowledge and the Living Word," will deal with the matter of epistemology, or our knowledge of God, as it emerges from the doctrine of justification by faith. It will seek to show that the knowledge of God which brings life to man is not merely knowledge about God, but is an entering into covenant with God, and that this is the meaning of *faith* in the doctrine of justification by faith. The tendency in the church today to which this treatment of epistemology has relevance is the tendency to teach about God as though he were the object of intellectual inquiry rather than the source of life itself.

Chapter two, "No Easy Sainthood," will deal with the biblical doctrine of man, which includes the doctrines of sin and salvation as these are required by the doctrine of justification by faith, describing the church's way of dealing with ourselves and our fellow men in view of the glory and the misery of man. The tendency in the church which may be corrected by taking seriously the doctrine of sin is the tendency to deal with people as though we could mold them into whatever pattern we wish, as though we were God to create man in our own image.

Chapter three, "We Are All Barabbas," is concerned with the problem of Christian ethics as this grows out of the doctrine of justification by faith. It describes the new life of the Christian as life in covenant with God and community with man, a life of forgiveness and freedom made possible as God's grace is made known through the church. The tendency in the church that may be modified by giving attention to the nature of Christian ethics is the tendency to teach moral axioms as though man can be good by merely deciding to do so.

Chapter four, "The New Creation," deals with the biblical view of history, with the church's call to participate with Christ, the living Lord of the church, in a movement toward communion and fellowship with all men everywhere about the feet of God. The tendency in the church to which this discussion is directed is the tendency to picture the Kingdom of God statically and propositionally as though God were doing nothing and going nowhere.

"Then the LORD answered Job out of the whirlwind: 'Who is this that darkens counsel by words without knowledge?' "

(Job 38:1-2)

CHAPTER ONE

Words Without Knowledge and the Living Word

The problem of Christian education is first of all the problem of how a person may be related to God, and what part is played in his relation to God by the various kinds of knowledge available to him. Once this is clear—once we are convinced that man can or cannot know God intimately and personally, that man does or does not have access to truth about God, that relationship to God does or does not depend on factual knowledge about him—then the church can develop a program of education with some assurance. But until this question is answered satisfactorily, the Christian educator can only fumble around, imitating secular education, and thus fall short of his distinctive task.

FAITH DEFINED AS MAN'S RESPONSE TO GOD'S REVELATION

The doctrine of justification by faith reflects the conviction of the Christian church that man can know God immediately and personally—indeed, that man's true destiny is the knowledge of God and communion with him. Moreover, the Protestant Reformation turned on the conviction that God has come seeking man to win man to himself and that man need do nothing more to assure his salvation than simply to trust in God's gracious gift. This very trust is the heart of the relationship that exists between man and God. It is the result of man's knowledge of God. Trust in God is for the Reformers the exact equivalent of knowledge of God. Moreover, trust, or faith, is man's response to God. It is called into being by God's revelation of himself to man. It does not therefore exist by man's effort, but comes to him as a gift of God. Faith is man's response to God's revelation and cannot be understood apart from an understanding of revelation. For the Christian faith starts from the fact that God has revealed himself to man in distinctive ways, calling man into communion with him, and that man's capacity to respond—indeed, the will to do so—is itself God's gift to man.

The tendency in the church to teach about God without making serious acknowledgment of the fact that man may know God himself personally and intimately is one of the disconcerting tendencies with which these reflections are concerned; for it grows out of a basic misunderstanding of the nature of the Christian faith and cuts the church off from the life-giving relationship with God which Jesus Christ came to make possible.

The actual message of the gospel of God made known in Jesus Christ is the message that God has come seeking man to draw him into fellowship with himself. This is the revelation from God, the self-disclosure of God. Man's faith in God is man's response to this gospel fact. When the church keeps this upper-most in its mind and heart, the church has a message that brings life to man. When the church gets confused about this elemental fact, the church's mission to the world becomes confused.

The Church's Confusion About the Meaning of Revelation

It is in fact the church's confusion about the meaning of these two concepts, revelation and faith, that has caused much of the difficulty in the educational work of the church. The question is: How does God make himself known to man, and how is man able to respond to God? How can the church pass down its faith in God so that in each generation the church may know God and find new life in him? If we can answer these questions in sufficiently large terms, we shall be able to establish the work of the church on a sounder basis. If we misunderstand these terms, or if we see them in too small a compass, the work of the church will continue to reflect this limitation and its people will continue to suffer spiritual malnutrition.

The point may be illustrated from a brief look at the way the church has understood the idea of revelation at certain stages in its history,[1] and the way it has in consequence understood its educational task.

During the Middle Ages the church generally understood revelation as a body of truth given by God to the church, a body of truth which contained what man should believe and how man should live. Holding this body of truth to be fixed and complete, the church believed its chief work to be the transmission of that body of truth from one generation to another. The fact that this body of truth might be empty words *about* God with no immediate, personal knowledge *of* God did not affect the church's commitment to the task.

The church of the Reformation, however, rejected this sterile concept of revelation because it remembered that revelation had come to man in the person of Jesus Christ, the Living Word. It sought to recover the living faith of the New Testament church, which knew firsthand this event in which God had come to meet man. "Faith," said Calvin, "does not merely believe about Christ; it embraces him with the soul."[2] "Doctrine is not an affair of the tongue, but of the life; it is not apprehended by the intellect and memory merely, like other branches of learning, but is received only when it possesses the whole soul, and finds its seat and habitation in the inmost recesses of the heart."[3]

But in spite of their dissatisfaction with the formalism of the Roman Church and the assurance that man may himself stand in the presence of God, the Reformers were limited by their interpretation of the Bible and were unable to get completely away from the concept of faith as assent to a body of truth found in the Bible. They did not develop systematically their doctrine of revelation, which might have led the church to a stronger and more consistent position. As a consequence the Protestant church has down through the years been handicapped by the ambiguities that have persisted at this very important point.

We may summarize the years since the Reformation in brief fashion by referring to two developments within the Protestant churches that have bearing on the problem of the meaning of revelation. One of these developments was the rise of Protestant scholasticism; the other was the rise of rationalism. Both fell far short of a strong view of revelation.

Protestant scholasticism followed hard on the heels of the creative period of the Reformation. The conviction that the Roman Church had wandered from the true faith led the Protestants to a large concern for a correct formulation of doctrine. Their opposition to the dependence of the Roman churches on the authority of the Pope caused them to move to a corresponding dependence on the authority of the Bible, with the result that they began to "treat the Bible as an external and objective standard," infallible at every point, the literal word of God. For this part of Protestantism and its spiritual descendants, the major educational responsibility of the church is understood as passing down a knowledge of the Bible.

The rationalism that developed in the eighteenth century as an expression of a modern spirit did not make the mistake of identifying revelation with the Scripture, as the Protestant scholastics did. Rather, the rationalists at last denied the fact of revelation altogether. With the increased appreciation for the intellectual faculties of man, the rationalists saw less and less need for revelation as a means of knowledge, and by the nineteenth century an important stream of liberal theologians found little or no use for revelation at all and substituted a vague emotional "religion" for the revealed truth of the Christian faith.

The influence of this nineteenth-century liberal theology upon twentieth-century developments in religious education is easily seen. The fact that religious education has been person-centered rather than gospel-centered is a natural consequence of the nineteenth century's concern for the dignity of man. The concern for moral values and the use of the Bible passages in piecemeal fashion to support these moral values rather than to speak its own message reflect the low estimate of Scripture. The hesitation to confront children with the supernatural aspects of the gospel story seems clearly to stem from the emphasis upon man as a rational being whose destiny is largely in his own hands. T. S. Eliot expresses for us the futility of this matter-of-fact assumption that human knowledge is all we have need of:

> The endless cycle of idea and action,
> Endless invention, endless experiment,
> Brings knowledge of motion, but not of stillness;
> Knowledge of speech, but not of silence;
> Knowledge of words, and ignorance of the Word.
> All our knowledge brings us nearer to our ignorance,
> All our ignorance brings us nearer to death,
> But nearness to death no nearer to GOD.
> Where is the Life we have lost in living?
> Where is the wisdom we have lost in knowledge?
> Where is the knowledge we have lost in information?
> The cycles of Heaven in twenty centuries
> Bring us farther from GOD and nearer to the Dust.[4]

Revelation Redefined in Biblical Theology

In the past few years, however, there has been a revolution in theology that has had a marked effect on the life of the church. Recent developments in biblical studies have opened the way to a more fruitful view of revelation and thus to a more fruitful understanding of the task of the church than has been reflected in the former work of the Protestant churches. This is not a new view of revelation in its essential outline. It may, indeed, be the dynamic view of revelation sought by the Reformers when they returned to the Bible for their authority, and it may enable us to establish the work of the church on the strong foundation the Reformers themselves wished to build.

This view of revelation is made possible by recent biblical

scholarship in what has been spoken of as the "post-critical" period of Bible study. This period is not to be thought of as "post-critical" in the sense of non-critical; actually it makes full use of all so-called critical processes available to Bible students. It uses them now with maturity, however, not simply to know *about* the Bible, but in order to arrive at the message of the Bible itself. This procedure has led the church to an understanding of revelation that throws further light on the nature and message of the Bible and that offers invaluable assistance in the transmission of the gospel.

One of the results of this "post-critical" study of the Bible is the recognition of the *unity* of the Bible. Although the Bible is composed of many kinds of literature, written by many persons, over a long period of time, nevertheless it is seen to be clearly one story—the story of God's work for man's salvation. Throughout the Bible, from Genesis to Revelation, God is at work seeking to establish covenant with man. The Old Testament is seen as a record of certain unique historical events through which God has made himself known to the Hebrew people. The New Testament is seen as the record of the life, death, and resurrection of Jesus Christ and the founding of the Christian church—another sequence of unique historical events in which God disclosed himself and his purpose to man. In the light of recent studies we may recognize revelation, then, as that which takes place when God comes to man and enters into man's life. Revelation is not simply information about God although it does bring new information about God. Revelation is God's presenting himself to man, inviting man to enter into life with him. Revelation is the meeting of God and man.

Our study of the Bible as a single, unified book has directed our attention also to the centrality of the covenant in God's dealing with man. The covenant is central to the story of the Bible, in the Old Testament as well as in the New, as the word "testament" or "covenant" implies. Revelation results in covenant. That is, God always comes to man as to one with whom he wishes to enter into a relationship of mutual faithfulness. God is not concerned to convey information merely for the sake of satisfying curiosity about his nature or his purpose, or providing for mystical aspiration. As Pascal puts it, "The *knowledge* of God is very far from the love of him." No person wants to be merely an object of intellectual inquiry or abstract worship to another person. God is concerned to enter into a profound and life-giving relationship with persons like himself who will receive him as their God and accept life from his hands.

The work of the church rests on its faith that God has come and continues to come to man in covenant in every generation and that he has entrusted to the church the responsibility for witnessing to this covenant. The church believes that in Jesus Christ God has spoken and still speaks, that in this One who is the culmination of his revelation God is inviting all men into covenant with him, extending fellowship to men, saying, "I will be your God. I want you for my people." Whatever the church does is to be done for extending his rule throughout the earth.

The Meaning of Faith

Faith, as it is intended in the doctrine of justification by faith, is man's response to God's revelation. Faith is man's acceptance of God's invitation to covenant. If revelation is the unveiling of God, the expression of God in a living Word, making known to man the living Christ, who is always present to man, then faith is man's opening of himself to God so that the living Christ may become enmanned in him.

The organic nature of this relationship thus established between God and man defies ordinary speech and makes it necessary to resort to symbols and dramatic imagery if man is to grasp the possibilities that lie before him. Religious truth of such dimensions must always be expressed in figurative language, the language of the emotions and the imagination. Through the years the Christian church has accumulated a wealth of figures of speech by which it expresses this most significant of man's relationships—his faith in Jesus Christ, or his response to God's Word. As is always true of figurative language, these images by which we try to describe faith fall short of adequate description. They merely point in the direction in which we shall find the reality. No figure is an adequate representation. The reality goes far beyond the normal meaning of the word, and only when our minds take flight in imagination can we glimpse that which is most real.

The variety of metaphors by which the church attempts to describe man's relation to God is very great and come from many areas of thought. No one image is an adequate representation of the truth. Each image points to one aspect of truth only and must be taken in relation to other figures before the truth it holds can be adequately grasped.

Sometimes we use sociological terms, and faith is seen as man's acceptance of God's invitation to come into God's family and to become a member of the household of God. When we use this figure, we recognize that the household encompasses the whole of God's creation and includes mankind of every generation and of every corner of the world. "Truly," says Calvin, "faith justifies us for no other reason than that it reconciles us to God, and this not by its own merit, but only because as we receive the grace offered to us in the promises and are certainly persuaded that we are loved by God as sons, we also come to possess the assurance of life eternal."[5]

Sometimes we use legal or commercial terms, and faith is seen as entering into covenant, trusting in God's faithfulness and pledging fidelity in return. When one of the partners of the covenant is God, however, we recognize that the character of covenant is changed, for God's faithfulness cannot be dependent on man's. Then the covenant, instead of being a legal contract as it is in human terms, becomes a covenant of grace and a basis of utter security for man.

Sometimes we use spiritual terms, in which case faith is seen as man's opening himself to God's own Spirit, to be indwelt and taken hold of by God's power and love. The New Testament is full of indications that God is willing—nay, is eager—to enter into man's own heart and transform and fulfill.

Justification by faith is itself a juridical figure taken from the law court. Although its use today seems to us technical and institutional, in New Testament times it was a figure that best expressed to the Jewish mind the unexplainable love of God for man in spite of the vast gulf that separated them. It was a way of saying that the righteousness of God was more akin to love than to retributive justice. It said to the disciples that God's feeling for man is compassion, that the quality above all other qualities that marks God is his unwarranted love for man.

Whatever figure we use to describe the relationship, we must remember that it is a figure only, a sign that points toward the kind of event that takes place when man meets God, when the created one stands awake, conscious of the event, in the presence of the Creator. Our pedestrian earth-bound words cannot exhaust the meaning of this which we call the revelation of God and man's response of faith. But this is the kind of meeting of God and man that the Reformers intended when they spoke of justification by faith.

It means that God created man in his own image in order to enter into fellowship with him; that man's chief end is to glorify God and enjoy him forever; that God, though he is unlimited, self-sufficient, complete in himself, wanting nothing, yet wants man to be his, wants to enjoy man and glorify him. Though man is a creature, brought into being out of nothing, yet God values him so much that he wants companionship with him and wants through companionship with him to enable him to become truly man. Though man in his present state is so unlike God as to be incompatible with God, unsuited in every respect for companionship with him, yet God reaches out to man in unwavering, unconditional love, and offers man life.

Emil Brunner in *The Divine Imperative* puts it this way: "Without any complementary human effort man receives, purely as a gift, that justification which he seeks in vain to attain for himself. The meaning of the whole doctrine of justification by faith—indeed, the meaning of the whole message of the Bible—is this: that it is not man's efforts by way of the Law—and the human way is always the way of the Law—but that God by the way of grace gives the true relation to God and therefore the true existence. For in its actual specific message the Bible does not deal with the God who demands and the man who acts, like every other sacred book; but it speaks of the God who acts and the man who receives the Divine gift."[6]

Faith, then, is man's openness to God, an openness that is made possible for man only because the compassion and love of God have been made known. Faith is man's trust in God. It finds confidence in God's abiding presence. Its security rests on its hope in God's eternal faithfulness.

The Heidelberg Catechism expresses this meaning of faith in its answer to Question Twenty-one: "What is true faith? It is not only a certain knowledge whereby I hold for truth all that God has revealed to us in His word, but also a hearty trust, which the Holy Ghost works in me by the Gospels, that not only to others, but to me also, forgiveness of sins, everlasting righteousness and salvation, are freely given by God, merely of grace, only for the sake of Christ's merits."[7]

The Church's Responsibility
to Communicate the Faith

On these terms the job of the church is to make God's grace known to man in order that man may open himself to God in faith and find life in communion with him, that man may enter into God's eternal purpose.

The church has two primary means or instruments—the Bible and the church's own life—by which it can make God's love known to man.

The Bible as Instrument of Communication

In the Bible the fact of God's love is made known in a story the church may tell. Here is set forth the story of God's coming to man, saying first to Abraham, then to his family and to Israel as a whole, and finally through Jesus Christ to the new Israel, the church, "I will be your God and you will be my people—and I will make of you a great nation, and through you will all people of the earth be blessed."

As the people of Israel told and retold this story as the story of their own life in covenant with God, the fact of God's grace was made plain to the nation. The story became their means of keeping alive their faith that they were God's people, and of communicating this faith to their children and to their children's children. The story was the record of their spiritual pilgrimage as they understood it. It was the record of great events in the nation's history which by means of the Spirit they knew as acts of God calling them to be his peculiar people.

But it was more than a record of past events. As they told the story to their children with burning intensity, aware that their very existence as a people depended on these events, the meeting of God and man took place again. This was no ordinary story. It was the medium through which God continued to speak to his people—witness to what he had done in the past, instrument through which the word of God came again and again and called them to be his people.

In the same way today the Christian church knows the Bible to be an instrument through which God still works to create a people with whom he can live. The events recorded in this book are not events that happened once and are forever gone. They are part of a living story the end of which is yet in the future. In the story itself, whenever man hears it, may be found the Word of God seeking the heart of man.

A man reads the Bible today and identifies himself with the people of God, whose story it is. As he does so the Word of God, who has been at work from the beginning, calls to the heart of the reader as he called to the heart of Abraham in Chaldea and to the heart of Paul on the Damascus Road. The words of Scripture become an eternally contemporary vehicle for the Living Christ, who is the Word of God. Christ uses these words and these stories to draw the reader into the household of God, where he may be one with all who have loved God. And the story of

God's work for man's redemption which was begun the day God
said, "Let there be light," moves into the life of the church today
as men read the story and hear God speak to them.

It is the responsibility of the church, then, to open the Bible
for its members in such a way that they may come to it in faith,
ready to hear God speak and in speaking to lead them into covenant. For the people of God must listen again and again to the
story of their life, how God took them when they were no people
and made them his people. And as they listen, the event occurs
again, and man meets God and is created anew.

The Church's Own Life as Instrument of Communication

The second instrument through which the church can make
known the message of God's grace is the church's own life.
Whereas in the Bible the revelation is made plain in a story, in
the church the witness is borne in relationships. The church is
the contemporary expression of the ongoing story. The church
is the body of Christ, the habitation of the Spirit. The church is
the continuing witness to the Word of God in the world today.

As the church worships God, celebrating the sacraments, listening to the Word of God, lifting its voice in confession and repentance; as it reflects the love of God in its own way of working
in office and field and factory, the Word of God is manifest to
the world again as a living Word, and man is called again to
enter into covenant with God and into community with man.
Thus the church bears witness to the fact that God has spoken
and a community of faith has been established.

This does not mean that it is the church which redeems. It
means simply that the church bears witness to the redeeming
work of God. The church cannot redeem; its own redemption is
far from complete. The church always bears about it and within
it the mark of the world as well as the mark of Christ, and many
a man of the world looks upon it in amazement that it can call
itself a church, and turns away from Christ because of the
church.

Nevertheless, the church is in its very existence a witness to the work of Christ, a fact of history that cannot be denied. With all of its infidelity to its covenant the church still stands as a testimony to the fact that God loves man even when man sabotages the Kingdom of God, that God will not let go even in the face of this infidelity.

And the church is the instrument through which the revelation is communicated to the world. The church is the eternally contemporary body of believers in whose life and worship the Word becomes alive. It propagates its faith by drawing into itself the men and women and boys and girls who are seeking God and by pointing continually to the Source of its own hope. As these come into the church and participate in its life, they too may become aware of the Living Lord of the church and may find themselves addressed by the Word of God calling them to life. As they are supported by the fellowship of the church which receives them into the body, they may be so strengthened that they can respond to God in faith and enter into covenant with him.

It is not enough, then, for the church to teach *about* its faith. The church must be continually aware of the fact that its mission is to provide the context and means by which man may himself meet God and in meeting him may find life. Everything the church does must be directed to that end. For the heritage of the church is a *living faith* which must be kindled anew in the heart of every individual. The church's responsibility in all of its life is to witness to God's revelation of himself in such terms as the church itself has experienced it, in order that the world may be led to recognize God's presence in the world and accept his love in trustful obedience.

THE TASK OF CHRISTIAN EDUCATION

In the light of the foregoing discussions of the nature of faith as man's response to God's acts of self-disclosure, and of the nature of the Bible and the church's own life as witness and instrument of revelation, the task of Christian education begins to come clear. The task of Christian education is the task of the church—to

lead persons into the presence of God in such a way that they
may respond to him with their whole hearts. In what sense it
is proper to speak of this as education at all it is now our task
to set forth.

The communication of the faith calls for a distinctive kind of
education that is similar to and different from general education
in several very significant ways.

1. In the first place, Christian education, like general education,
is responsible for the transmission of knowledge.

There is a body of fact which is necessary to understanding and
entering into the Christian faith. The gospel story is a story of
the events in history in which God disclosed to man his own
nature and purpose. One does not communicate the Christian
faith when one teaches of these events, but it may be that one
cannot communicate the Christian faith apart from the knowledge
of these events. The Bible story, the creeds of the church, the
nature and meaning of the sacraments—all of these are the matrix
of the Christian faith, the cradle in which it rests, the clothes
it wears. The objective of the church is to bring persons face to
face with God in such a way that he may redeem their lives. It has
no way of doing this except by bearing witness to its own meeting
with God, telling again and again of the many forms this encounter has taken, describing the response that was called forth in
them. Believing as it does that God is forever seeking the heart
of man, the church seeks to arouse in the heart a sensitiveness to
God's presence, a willingness to listen for his word and to respond.
So the church tells how its own heart has been opened. It tells
what happened when Abraham listened to the voice of God, how a
covenant was established when Moses saw a burning bush, how a
church spread through the Mediterranean when Saul was struck
blind on the Damascus road! And it hopes that this telling may
open the way for another encounter to take place, and for other
great redemptive movements to begin.

It must teach the history of the church, its origin in the Bible
story, its nature as the body of Christ, its mission in the world
as the instrument of the Suffering Servant, in order that its mem-

bers may enter with understanding into the life of the church. The worship and work of the church must reflect the Lord of the church and the story of the church. The historical and eschatological character of the church must inform its expressions, providing the norm for the church's life.

2. In the second place, Christian education, like general education, has certain skills to teach as well as certain information to impart. The skills are those required for full participation in the life and work of the church, the skills that enable one to lay hold on the data of the faith and enter into faith.

An individual who would know God as he has revealed himself in Christ needs skill in Bible study—an understanding of the nature of the Bible and a knowledge of principles of biblical interpretation. One of the convictions of the Protestant church that has been preserved for us from Reformation days is that the Bible should be an open book so that everyone may read for himself the message of God's grace.

It is not that the Bible is in itself redemptive, however. The church does not regard the book as the agent of salvation. But the church has discovered that whenever a person comes to the Bible reading it in the faith that it is the book of the people of God, the Holy Spirit, who is the agent of redemption, speaks through the words of the Bible directly to the heart of man. So the church must "teach" this book, and develop in its members skill in reading the book, in order that the free Word of God may find an avenue through which it may speak to man.

An individual needs skill and understanding in worship, and particularly in the sacraments. The church has established forms of worship by means of which it expresses adoration, thanksgiving, and petition as the people of God. The church knows that no form of worship is of itself either necessary to or a guarantee of salvation. But it has received from its Lord certain sacraments and it has inherited from its forebears certain forms through which its relationship to God may be clearly expressed, and it has found that in these sacraments and forms persons are likely to be drawn into the presence of God. So the church must "teach" its members to participate with understanding in these acts of worship in the hope that as they enter together into these acts of worship, they may together meet God and find life in him.

The church must teach these things not only with reticence but with diligence. It must teach with reticence because it knows that nothing the church can do or say carries life, and it has no guarantee that the Spirit will act in certain ways and under certain circumstances. But it must teach with diligence because it has come to know that the Word and the sacraments are means the Spirit of God has often used as means of his grace, and will surely use again.

3. In the third place, Christian education like general education feels a responsibility for personal growth and for changes in behavior and attitudes. A disciple of Christ is expected to be different because of his allegiance to Christ. He has been promised the Spirit of Christ in his heart and looks forward to being transformed into the likeness of Christ. "It is no longer I who live, but Christ who lives in me,"[8] the Apostle Paul could say; and every Christian yearns for this same identification with the Christ. So, although the church is not the effective agent of change, it may, like any school, anticipate change in its members as they go through its educational program.

The change to be anticipated when men meet God may be thought of in two parts although the two parts are actually inseparable except for purposes of analysis. The first and most significant is the change that is brought about in man from without by the power of God acting upon his heart. The second is a volitional change in which man himself is the actor by the grace of God. This is man's attempt to bring his behavior in line with what he now knows himself to be—namely, the child of God.

In the first of these the church's role can hardly be referred to as "educational," for the church simply serves as channel for the grace of God which it has itself known and now expresses to another. This change is the change that takes place when love takes hold of a man. It is a change so far out of his own control that he can express it only by saying in bashful amazement, "It happened to me." In the second the church deliberately undertakes to help man discover what grace requires and makes possible in this situation in which he now lives. "Now that this has happened to me, how shall I behave at this point, and this?"

The Word of God comes to men in the situations in which they live and demands response in terms of personal relationships in these situations; therefore, the church must assist its members to discover the nature of the changed behavior required by the gospel in today's world. This is without question an educational task calling for a realistic appraisal of the society of which they are a part, for honest acceptance of responsibility where they are in a measure responsible for corruption and injustice, for a willingness to attack evil at those spots where change can be effected. The church cannot assume that men of faith will automatically know the demands of obedience to God, or that they will be able to follow Christ without hesitation. All too often Christian men and women have been content with good intentions and have neglected the honest and often difficult study necessary for understanding what is called for by devotion to Christ in the twentieth century. The church must therefore not only point to Christ as the source of grace, but must teach Christian ethics in a responsible way, setting forth both the promise of redemption and a method of dealing with problems of life under the Lordship of Christ.

The task of Christian education, then, is a unique task, as is made clear when looked at in the light of the key doctrine of the Protestant Reformation, justification by faith. Christian education is designed to bring about the relationship between man and God which the church knows as faith. This is a relationship which depends on the nature of God as Redeemer and Father and which is called forth in response to God's self-disclosure of his love. The church has come to know faith—indeed, the church has always known faith—as an intimately personal response to God's act of grace, an entering into covenant with One who always comes offering covenant. The church's program of education is simply the church's effort to make known to every man that he—like all mankind—is included in the purposes of God and called into his family. Whatever the church can do to bring men into such knowledge of God may be known as Christian education.

"For it is the God who said, 'Let light shine out of darkness,' who has shone in our hearts to give the light of the knowledge of the glory of God in the face of Christ."
(2 Corinthians 4:6)

CHAPTER TWO

No Easy Sainthood

The system of theology of which justification by faith is the organizing principle rests not only on the doctrine of God's grace, but also on a doctrine of man as image of God and sinner, created for fellowship with God but unable of himself to enter into that fellowship. It is our task in this chapter to look more closely at this doctrine of man—that is, at the church's belief about ourselves—in order to see what bearing it has on the life and work of the church.

It is my conviction that in its educational work, indeed in all of its work, the church largely ignores the doctrine of sin and the image of God, and that herein lies the seat of much of the church's difficulty and the reason for the sub-Christian character of its life. Because of this the church is prone to undertake tasks it has no fitness for and to fail in the distinctive tasks for which it was created. Without stopping to ask what man is like or what power is needed for change, the church sets out to bring about a complete transformation in man. But the nature of man is such that no human being has the power to change another. The church is itself always in need of change and can act in the redemption of the world only as God is willing to work through the church.

Perhaps if we can come closer to understanding the biblical
doctrine of man—that is, of ourselves—we will come closer to
discovering an appropriate way for us to communicate the Christian faith to other people like ourselves, drawing them to God,
who alone can bring about a change in man. In chapter one
we looked at the nature of the faith to be communicated. In
this chapter we shall look at the nature of man to whom the faith
is to be conveyed, recognizing that as we do so we are looking at
ourselves as well as those to whom we are to minister through
the work of the church.

THE BIBLICAL DOCTRINE OF MAN

Two distinct and apparently contradictory elements make up
the biblical doctrine of man, as has been recognized by Christian
theology throughout the years. These two elements have been
described dramatically for us in the words of David Roberts, as
"the grandeur and the misery of man."[1] The doctrine of justification by faith requires full recognition of both of these elements.

The Grandeur of Man

The grandeur of man is that he has been created in the image
of God. The church acknowledges this fact, and glories in it, but
what it means the church has been trying to discover for centuries.
Certainly it means at least that we are creatures. We are not self-
sufficient. We are not the ultimate. We did not call ourselves
into being but were brought into being by someone else. We
simply found ourselves in existence. The most important factors
in our lives were not our choice; they happened to us. We thus
owe our existence and the nature of our being to someone else
more powerful than ourselves.

But the fact that we were created means that someone wanted
us, each of us, enough to fashion us as we are. Each one of us
is unique, different from all other persons. We are surprised when
someone says to us, "Has anyone ever told you that you look just

like John Jones?" We are even a little disconcerted by the thought
that someone else was created just like us.

And yet the opposite is also true of us. Sometimes we find it
difficult to accept the uniqueness of ourselves, and we rebel
against being this particular thing that God has created. We wish
we had hair of another color, or we wish we were not so tall, or
we would like to have been born with more brains, or more money.
We overlook the fact that we are created the beings we are
because the Creator wanted us to be this.

Not only were we created, but we were created in the image
of God. Although we are akin to the rest of the created world in
many respects, we cannot finally be described in terms of animals,
with which of all created things we have the most in common.
God has created us more like himself than like anything else in
the world. This is the great heritage of man.

Moreover, early in the biblical record we find man in fellowship
with God. This is our glory, that we were made not for life with
the animals but for life with God, for communion with God. Man
is one to whom God says, "Thou"; who, though not self-sufficient
but given his life by another, is called into his true being by his
own response to God's Word to him. This, if the Westminster
Shorter Catechism is correct, is the meaning of human nature—
that man should enter into life with God, to glorify and enjoy him.
This is our destiny, our "chief end." Failure to understand this
high doctrine is the root of the humanism that marks all too much
of the program of the church today.

The glory of man, of ourselves, is that God created us in God's
own image in order that we might enter into fellowship with him.
The glory of man is that God in Christ took upon himself our
image in order that our fellowship with God might be realized.
The glory of man is that through Christ we are to be raised to
God's image, and the oneness of God with us and of ourselves with
God is to be made complete. Whenever we try to define human
nature in any other terms we get in trouble.

The salvation of man—the high destiny of man—can never
be defined in terms of things (golden streets, or star-studded

crowns), or in terms of man's own self (his moral perfection, or the fullest development of his self), or in terms of other men (the good society). Salvation is to be defined in terms of the fellowship with God for which man was created. Salvation is life lived in the covenant family of God. Within this fellowship all other things follow: In fellowship with God, man is brought to his fullest development. In the presence of God, streets are paved with gold. In covenant with God, one lives in community with one's fellows. But these are by-products of the essential fact, and impossible except in relation to the essential fact.

The grandeur of man is that he is created in the image of God, for fellowship with God. As such he is endowed with the capacity for communicating with God, and is of such a nature that he does not fulfill his destiny unless he is in communion with God. It is man's essential nature to live with God and with his fellow man. When living in fellowship with God, man is himself. He lives freely and joyously. He moves toward maturity. When out of fellowship with God, he is out of line with his true nature, in disharmony with the created world, and in discord with man. His behavior is a continual source of confusion and chaos.

Another factor in the character of man that is made plain in the Bible is that man is a unit.[2] He is one. He is not made up of many different parts that can be taken apart and put together at will. Man is not a body plus a soul plus a mind. He is always all three. Every part of man depends on every other part and affects every other part. God created the whole and means that it shall operate as a whole.

But the oneness of man has a larger meaning even than this. An individual man is not only a single unit in himself; he is also a part of a larger unity with all mankind. This is seen on a smaller scale in groups of persons with whom we have any kind of relationship—a family, a community, a nation. If any one person is taken out of such a group, the entire group is diminished, impoverished. In a very real sense whatever happens to one of the group happens to the group as a whole. Whatever any one of the group does, the whole group does. The Bible makes it clear that there is a corporate guilt for the evil of any one person. This is expressed in the story of the Fall, in which the sin of Adam is taken as the sin of all mankind. We partake of one another.

This concept of unity takes on particular significance when in the New Testament we read of being in Christ, of Christ dwelling in us, of our being members of the body of Christ. We read in the high priestly prayer of Christ the purpose of God for all mankind. "That they may all be one; even as thou, Father, art in me, and I in thee, that they also may be in us."[3] We catch here a glimpse of the meaning of image of God and fellowship with God —that to be created a man is to be created in order that we may be bound together with God, participating in his life, sharing his life with all mankind.

What God wants of man is that he shall acknowledge himself as a member of the family of God, and only this. His attitude toward man is like that of a father toward a child whom he would like to adopt as his own son. All he wants is acceptance, communion. God comes to man offering communion freely, no matter what man is like at this time. This communion is not offered as a reward for goodness. It is freely offered companionship of father and son. This is the essential meaning of the doctrine of justification by faith, that God comes to man in grace, inviting man to live with him, and participate in him.

Man does not have to be perfect in order to accept this invitation to belong to God. He is not even expected to be perfect at this stage of life. God knows better than we that man is finite, created, still becoming what he is to be. "He knoweth our frame; he remembereth that we are dust." But he loves us anyway. This does not mean that righteousness is unimportant. It merely means that righteousness is not to be defined as simply meeting a standard. Righteousness is characteristic of Being itself, of God himself. It is necessary to fullness of life, or to life in God. Righteousness is another word for love; it is made possible only in relationship with one who is himself righteous. One learns to love only by being loved, deeply and profoundly.

The essential characteristic of God, made plain in Jesus Christ, is that God loves like that; God is willing to give himself in love to man, knowing that man can learn to enter into fellowship only when he has known fellowship of this kind. What God wants is for man to live with him and with all mankind as a family of persons mutually in love, given to the service of one another.

The Misery of Man

The misery of man is the difficulty man has in entering into fellowship with God. Sin has been defined in many ways, but perhaps the most helpful definition we can give is inordinate self-love, or the inability to love another and to enter into true fellowship with another, whether God or man.[4]

The doctrine of sin gives the church great difficulty, and, while a familiar term to the preacher, it has been almost completely neglected in all parts of the church's life except the pulpit. Sin has been simply a doctrine for the church to preach about, rather than a condition of man to take into account in the church's program. The church must think more carefully into the biblical doctrine of man, the doctrine of sin and the new life, and let these doctrines govern the whole of its life and work. It must recognize that sin is not a doctrine only, but a fact. Calvin Coolidge's story about the preacher who was "against sin" is true of the whole church. We are against it and can argue heatedly about it, but we can seldom come to any agreement about its implications for our lives. All too often we dismiss it because we cannot get hold of it in a neat theological formula with which we can deal.

Even so great a theologian as St. Augustine was confused about the nature of sin, although his statement of the nature of sin was one of the most profound statements we have. Augustine was completely unwilling to agree to the Pelagian doctrine of sin as man's failure to live up to moral laws. Augustine was convinced that sin is a universal characteristic rooted deep in man's very being. From this he drew the conclusion that sin is "natural" to man, or part of God's work of creation; and in so saying he destroyed man's responsibility for his behavior and left the burden of sin upon God. He found the same difficulty that we find—the difficulty of defining sin in sufficiently universal and sufficiently profound terms to account for its devastating effects upon human nature, and at the same time defining it in terms of man's responsibility for his own evil deeds.[5] To follow either Augustine or Pelagius uncritically is to do violence to one phase or another of the biblical doctrine of sin.

In the famous controversy between these two may be found the seeds of the church's confusion about the nature of sin. Elements of truth and elements of untruth may be found in both camps. Sin is a state of the soul for which man is in a sense not responsible and from which he must be delivered, but it is at the same time an act of infidelity for which man is responsible and for which he must acknowledge his guilt. Sin is an individual matter and at the same time a social responsibility.

The Bible reflects many aspects of sin and makes no attempt to reconcile them into one consistent theory. On the one hand there are the prophets denouncing the children of Israel for their unfaithfulness. On the other hand there is the psalmist crying out, "Wash me thoroughly from my iniquity, and cleanse me from my sin!" On the one hand, the tables at Sinai warn that God will visit the iniquity of the fathers upon the children, and on the other Jeremiah proclaims that everyone shall die for his own iniquity.

Whereas the philosophers struggle with the nature of evil, its origin and source, the biblical writers do not attempt to formulate a systematic and completely logical doctrine. The Bible accepts the fact of sin as rooted deep in the most elemental relationships of man, and spends its energies in telling of God's cure for sin. This as a matter of fact is the only way in which evil can be dealt with. Even the most persistent philosopher must finally give up his attempt to systematize, for if he takes evil seriously he always finds a surd evil which refuses to yield to logic. The danger of trying to philosophize or theologize about evil lies in the fact that in reducing evil to an intellectual problem we tend to ignore it as an existential problem. This is what the church is always tempted to do. The very ability to recite the answer to Question Fourteen of the Westminster Shorter Catechism gives us a sense of relief that now sin is well taken care of, and so we move on to the next question unaware that we have laid a trap for ourselves and fallen squarely into it.

For just as we found in chapter one that God is not simply a neat formula to be memorized and repeated back to the teacher, but is a living Person seeking man in eternal covenant love, so we must acknowledge in this chapter that sin is not simply a formula but a powerful gripping force, a soul-destroying predicament from which man must be delivered. It appears in man as estrangement from other men and thus from God. It is an organic disturbance in the very center of our being, a malignancy in our most basic relationships which reaches out and corrupts everything it touches. It is like a living thing which fastens itself on the soul. "Who will deliver me," cried Paul, "from this body of death?" The church would do well to forego the effort to take hold of sin logically, for sin continues to defy us with its illogic. We are always in danger, when we intellectualize sin, that we will deceive ourselves into thinking we are its master. "The mystery of iniquity," says T. S. Eliot, "is a pit too deep for mortal eyes to plumb."

The misery of man is that, created a person with capacity to think and to purpose and to love, he finds himself unaccountably shackled by some nameless power so that he can do none of this as he would and yet is unaccountably burdened by a sense of his guilt that he cannot. Here is a young woman we may call Kathleen, crippled in her very heart by her father's arrogance and brutality and by her mother's obvious preference for her sister, hungry for affection and unable to trust the friendship of anyone, building her shell more solidly about herself lest she be hurt more deeply than she can bear, and condemning herself cruelly because she is unable to meet the needs of children in the mission across town.

To recognize that the label "sin" must be attached to this deep hurt in Kathleen which makes it impossible for her to trust either God or man although she yearns for both, is to recognize the tragic irrational aspects of man's bondage, and the measure of our own responsibility for the bitter suffering sin brings to man.

The Offer of New Life

The two contradictory elements in man's life—his grandeur and his misery—are reconciled in the Bible only through God's offer of new life in Christ Jesus. Here it is made plain that the destiny of man can be fulfilled and his misery overcome by God's reconciling act. God comes to man, who is unable to come to him. God partakes of man, lays aside his Godhood to enter into manhood, in order that man may be able to partake of God and of his fellow men, entering into the unity for which he was created.

This is God's covenant promise to man, that he will be faithful, his pledge of security that the oneness he offers man does not depend on contingencies of any kind, his guarantee of unconditional fellowship. Within this covenant promise lies man's hope of salvation. Here is a community of love in which man's life can be nurtured.

Within this life in the family of God, man, who is becoming what he is to be, is brought into living relationship with that One Who Is. Here the transforming love of God can take hold of man and bring him to fulfillment. Outside of the family of God, man is cut off from God's love and removed from the possibility of salvation. As he lives with God, accepting his place as beloved son of the Father, he is set free from himself and comes to choose the Father's purposes as his purposes, the Father's values as his values. Recognizing that God has spent himself without reservation for him in his unworthiness, he is released from his own inordinate self-love and learns to give himself in mutual interdependence with the brother, as God gives himself to meet the needs of man.

Fellowship with God and man, for which we were brought into being, requires the surrender of the self to the other; and this we are simply unable to do until we are secure enough to trust. Love is a pouring out of one's self; an opening of one's self in utter abandon; a covenant promise of faithfulness to the other no matter what. A life of fellowship or love requires of us that which we cannot give until it has first been given us. Until I know beyond the shadow of a doubt that what I have to offer will be joyously received, I cannot give it. As long as I regard myself as unacceptable I must hold back. Made for love, a creature whose very existence as a person depends on love, I cannot love until I know myself to be loved.

THE CHURCH'S ATTEMPTS TO ESCAPE THE BIBLICAL DOCTRINE OF MAN

The basic question the church must ask about sin is not "How is sin to be defined?" or "What is the origin of sin?" The basic question is, "How is the church to deal with the reality of sin and the new life in the lives of men and women and boys and girls?"

In seeking an answer to this question it is important to recognize the many temptations that come to the church to escape the reality of sin and to look to the prospect of easy sainthood. There are three such temptations that the church falls prey to: intellectualism, legalism or moralism, and perfectionism. Each of these results from an unwillingness on the part of the church to admit the radical nature of sin and the real possibility of new life in Christ.

Intellectualism

Intellectualism is the temptation of all confessional churches (not excluding Presbyterians). Having accepted a particular confession as the authorized statement of our faith, we tend to assume that assent to the confession is the equivalent of faith. It results in a distortion of the doctrine of justification by faith, for it regards confessional orthodoxy as the meaning of faith and the condition of salvation. It holds that without assent to the confession there is no justification, but that salvation follows instantaneously upon assent to the confession. This is obviously a form of salvation by works and a denial of the very fact of grace the doctrine was intended to describe.

Intellectualism is a distortion of the nature of faith. It deals with faith as a gnosis, as though knowledge in itself has transforming power. "Faith," says Calvin, "has its seat not in the ears but in the heart . . . it is not enough to know that Christ was crucified and rose from the dead, unless we know these things in our lives. . . . We know Christ in the right way when we experience the meaning of his death and resurrection within us and as they become effective in us."[6]

Legalism or Moralism

The second temptation is the temptation to legalism or moralism. Legalists and moralists are Pelagian in their doctrine of man. They have a shallow conception of sin as man's willful violation of the law, thus denying sin as a soul-destroying power which fastens itself upon man to negate all possibility of community. They misread the gospel message and set up requirements for man by which they measure his righteousness, assuming with Socrates that if man knows the right he can easily perform it—and God will bless him if he does.

But moralism betrays the churchman into the sly hypocrisy of setting up standards to which he and his kind can measure up without great difficulty and of defining sin in terms which hold no sway over himself. Moralism leads to Pharisaism, which sets up walls of exclusiveness between the righteous who conform to standards and the sinners who do not. Dietrich Bonhoeffer gives us the lesson of the Pharisee in a sharp, clear way in an essay entitled The Pharisee: "The Pharisee is not an adventitious historical phenomenon of a particular time. He is the man to whom only the knowledge of good and evil has come to be of importance in his entire life; in other words, he is simply the man of disunion. Any distorted picture of the Pharisees robs Jesus's argument with them of its gravity and its importance. The Pharisee is that extremely admirable man who subordinates his entire life to his knowledge of good and evil and is as severe a judge of himself as of his neighbour to the honour of God, whom he humbly thanks for this knowledge."[7] The moralist misinterprets the Bible, reading it as a book of examples of righteous men and women who are to be imitated in life today, or as a book of laws which are to be rigidly obeyed. Thus in a teaching program illustrations are given and verses are quoted in an effort to get children to share their toys with one another, or to compel men to give a tithe of their goods to the church. But a church that has fallen prey to moralism does not know that until the grace of God takes hold of a human heart, man is unable to give himself to his brother; or that the gift of self is the only gift anyone wants and the only gift a human being has to give to either God or man.

Legalism or moralism denotes an unwillingness to admit man's finitude and sin and a lack of faith in God's power to redeem. The legalistic church tends to define the Christian life in terms of petty sins to be avoided and petty virtues to be emulated. It either does not understand the larger dimension of life that the biblical writers knew, or it is frightened by it. Legalism does not recognize the cosmic significance of hatred. It does not dare even to think of the new being or the new creation.

Perfectionism

A third temptation which besets the church—and this is the most subtle and dangerous of them all—is perfectionism or developmentalism. This is the belief that the goal of the church's work is the fullest development of the individual. It rests upon three fallacies about God and man: first, that a human being can be brought to fulfillment by the efforts of another human being; second, that a human being can anticipate the kind of person another human being can or should become; third, that the ultimate purpose of God can be stated in terms of individual perfection.

Perfectionism leads the church to set up goals in terms of precise character traits or behavior patterns and to push its people toward the accomplishment of these. It leads us directly back to the human striving to do something for God rather than to accept that which God has done for us. The center of the Bible's message, Emil Brunner says, is that God alone is good and that that alone is good which God does.[8]

A contemporary theologian, Cherbonnier, points out the danger of perfectionism in his book *Hardness of Heart*: "As the history of Pharisee and Puritan proves, there is nothing more fatal to human relations (and, we may add, to man's relation to God) than the man whose primary concern is to establish his own moral goodness."[9]

This is humanism and not gospel. This is a development to be expected in the twentieth century, when man's achievements lie in the area of the "man sciences" as well as in the conquest of outer space. It is the most insidious enemy the church has, because it is plausible and sophisticated. The church's alliance with contemporary psychology and progressive education has betrayed it into this idolatry. Its unwillingness to take seriously the universality and profundity of man's sin and the real possibility of new life in Christ has supported the betrayal.

THE IMPLICATIONS OF THE BIBLICAL DOCTRINE OF MAN FOR THE EDUCATIONAL WORK OF THE CHURCH

A consideration of the biblical doctrine of man reveals several implications for the educational work of the church.

The Church's Responsibility to Acknowledge Its Own Sin

The first implication of the biblical doctrine of man for the work of the church is the fact of sin in ourselves as in all other persons. Man does not cease to be a sinner when he comes into the church. The judgment of God is still upon him. He still sins and falls short of the calling for which he is called. The righteousness of God into which he is called is not diminished, nor does man approximate it in this life. It is to church members that Paul writes when he says, "Stop that stealing."

Justification does not mean that man is suddenly transformed into a saint upon acceptance of Jesus Christ. It simply means that he is now a member of the household of faith, that he is forgiven. The difference between the church member and the one who is not a church member is simply that the church member knows that he is forgiven. He has accepted God's forgiveness with a sense of its full cost to God. He has entered into the New Covenant of Christ's blood, accepting the sacrifice that has been given for him and aware of his utter unworthiness of the place given him in the family of God.

Karl Barth says, "We live by forgiveness." Although we know we fall short of obedience to God, we can exist because we have assurance of his grace. Moreover, we no longer have to pretend a holiness we do not have. We can acknowledge our subtle arrogance, our little deceits, our eagerness to escape responsibility, and all the rest of our sins.

This means that the church may not set itself apart from the world as though the church is better than the world and has the power to change the world. God's covenant with his people is a covenant of grace, a universal covenant intended for all men, because God wants it so and not because man deserves it. The preacher and the teacher are sinners, as the humblest members are, and as the prostitute down the street is. The preacher differs from the prostitute primarily in that he knows where forgiveness may be found. "Evangelism," says D. T. Niles, "is one beggar showing another beggar where to find bread."

The willingness to acknowledge one's own sin, made possible by the knowledge of God's grace, may create a situation in which the church can be heard by the world as the world cannot hear when the church stands off with clean skirts pulled around it and a purposeful look in its eye. Now a learning situation may be established for the first time, for the distance between teacher and learner is reduced if not altogether eliminated.

Teaching can never be defined as simply telling the learner the profound truth the teacher has learned. Nor is teaching simply pointing the learner to where truth may be found. Teaching requires the teacher and pupil to join hands and go out in search of truth together, the pupil set free to search by the teacher's respect for him and confidence in him. The teacher identifies himself with the learner, and is himself ready to learn.

So the gospel can never be taught as though it were an exclusive possession of the church. Teaching the gospel is a proclamation of the Good News of God and thus an invitation to come and stand in his presence and hear him speak what he will. The teacher does not create the gospel, nor does he discover it. The teacher does not control the gospel. On the other hand, the teacher is himself created by the gospel, discovered by it, controlled by it. Its word to him is never complete. He is always listener and learner.

Thus the teacher who can acknowledge his own predicament, his finitude and sin, stands always beside his pupil in the presence of God. He bears witness to the gospel he knows and has known, but he also bears witness to gospel he has yet to grasp and be grasped by. He listens with his pupil to what God would say to them together, and he listens in solitude to what God says to him as teacher alone.

This means that the teacher can teach now with humility and boldness. He can say what he knows, and can say it from his heart, conscious that he does not have to know everything. He is relieved of the awful necessity to be an authority with unshakable knowledge of what he is called to teach. He can now join hands with his pupil and go out asking questions and listening for answers. A class can explore together the implications of the gospel for their own lives, each one "teacher" in turn, each one always learner. The bitter rivalry that characterizes those who do not know the secret of God's grace is now removed. The fear of losing face is gone, for each one wears his own face no longer, but all wear the face of Christ. A band of self-acknowledged sinners can listen together to the Word of God and search fearlessly for its meaning for their lives, supporting one another in the search, reaching out to include any other sinner who may wish to come.

The Church's Responsibility to Recognize the Nature of Sin

The second implication of the biblical doctrine of man for the educational work of the church is that the church must recognize the complex nature of sin.

On the one hand, sin is devastating and reprehensible. It eats like a cancer into the soul of man, making him a power for the infection of other souls and for the annihilation of brotherhood. One has only to look at the wave of hatred and violence that has swept over our country since May, 1954, to recognize the malignancy of sin and the utterly irrational nature of prejudice and hatred. One has only to look at the bitter loneliness of Jesus Christ on the cross, put there *by* man's sin and *for* man's sin, to realize that even God draws back at the sight of sin.

On the other hand, we have the evidence also found in the Bible that sin is not a word of condemnation of another, but a word by which we can interpret man's distress and God's grace. The word "sin" is a word to be used only by those who have faith in God. It means rebellion against God. The one who uses the word "sin" refers to evil in its cosmic significance. He points to the fact that man's behavior has meaning far beyond man's intent. He is saying that all of us are caught in a web of evil from which we cannot extricate ourselves, but from which God wills to rescue us all. "Sin" is therefore necessarily a word of tenderness and compassion, a word that acknowledges our common humanity and our common need for redemption.

Because sin is a word that can be used only by those who have faith in God, it requires that when we use it we take into account God's relation to sin. The church cannot talk responsibly about sin apart from what it knows of God's attitude toward sin—that is, that God stands ready to forgive. Within the church the word "sin" has as its correlate the word "grace," and is not to be used apart from the message of God's grace. As judgment and mercy are correlates so are sin and grace.

Therefore within the church sin is always to be dealt with within the context of forgiveness. A child born into the church is a child of the covenant, a child who is forgiven. Within the community of those who have learned the meaning of grace by having faced their sin and received forgiveness, the child can learn to deal with sin in his own life. Long before he can learn to say the word "grace" or can verbalize the meaning of forgiveness or atonement, he can come to know through experience the fact that God judges and atones for sin.

Thus a teacher or preacher must examine his own conception of sin and his attitude toward it, lest his way of dealing with sin should serve to aggravate it in his pupils or his parishioners rather than enable them to deal with it adequately. All too often we have assumed that it is the teacher's or preacher's role to condemn sin roundly, and to exhort the listeners to abandon sin and to live good moral lives. The paradox of sin is that a broad condemnation of sin and exhortation to righteousness may only intensify the predicament. Moralistic teaching and preaching miss the point, overlooking the very nature of man. If it be true that man cannot save himself from his predicament, but must be lifted from his distress by Christ, the church should preach grace. To hear the law only drives me deeper into despair. No alcoholic is helped by a sermon on temperance. He requires a deep inner change that can be brought about only by an experience of profound and steadfast love such as has been made known in Jesus Christ and experienced by the church.

The church's own experience should have taught the church this way of dealing with sin. The church was brought into existence by the deep compassion of Christ for man's low estate into which he had fallen. Christ looked right through the symptoms of sin in man—the greediness of Zacchaeus, the infidelity of Peter, the fatuousness of the Samaritan woman—and spoke to the heart of the suffering men and women he saw there. His condemnation was reserved for those we call Pharisees, who denounced the immoral deed without a thought of the tragic need that prompted it.

In setting us free from sin, Christ set us free from this most devastating sin of them all—the moralism and legalism we so often substitute for the Christian faith, directing it now against ourselves in unbelief, directing it now against another in hypocrisy. Justification by faith is the church's conviction, more often declared than believed, that Christ did not come into the world to condemn the world but that the world through him might be saved.

This conviction requires a teacher, preacher, and parent to be sensitive to the need of others, listening to their distress, seeking the source of their grief. Our temptation is to one-way preaching, never entering into dialogue with the one we seek to help, wondering why men turn away from the gospel which we know to be the source of life. We are not afraid to preach to people or "teach" them, but we fear to talk seriously with individuals about the deepest concerns of life and death, afraid on the one hand that we may uncover a problem in the other too difficult for us to handle, afraid on the other hand that we may reveal to him a need in ourselves we are unable to face. Our problem in both cases is our unwillingness to look at sin for what it is and to look at ourselves as sinners.

In its educational program the church must take account of the universality of sin and its deep malignant nature so terrifying to us that we seldom face it in ourselves and others. The teacher must not be content to use words about sin whose meaning he does not take the pains to understand. The one factor that brought about the Protestant Reformation more than any other was Martin Luther's stubborn refusal to give up until he found the reality for which the church had shown him only symbols. The strength of the Protestant church—the only factor that will enable it to endure—is this insistence on going, at whatever cost, behind words and forms to the truth within. Theology is not a creed to be repeated only. Theology is an expression of man's relation to God. Its words have reference to the deep realities of human existence, and call us to move beyond the surface into the depths where human life is lived with God.

We are theologians. Whether we have an articulate theology or an adequate theology or not, we all have some theology. The value of a creed to us is twofold: It gives us the words which the church has found adequate over the years to express the profound experience once it has known it; and it may serve to arouse anticipation of the experience that others have known and to lead toward it, drawing the individual into the faith of the church in anticipation that the faith may become his own. The danger of a creed is that it may serve as substitute for faith rather than an affirmation of faith or a movement toward it.

The Church's Responsibility to Accept Its Ministry of Grace

The third implication of the Christian doctrine of man is that the church must accept the ministry of grace to which it is called as the body of Christ. Once the church has understood the doctrine of sin as an interpretation of man's tragic predicament and of his dire need for healing and reconciliation, once it has grasped the truth of the gospel that God does not condemn sin but judges it in order that he may redeem, the church knows no barrier between itself and the world. The exclusiveness that is aggravated by a moralistic or legalistic approach to life is eliminated by the recognition of our common humanity and the universality of God's grace. Barriers between saint and sinner are broken down. Knowing itself to exist in covenant only on the grace of God, the church accepts the stewardship of grace to which it has been called. The church is driven to adopt God's own attitude to the sinner—the attitude of compassion for one caught in predicament, and of yearning for community with him.

More than that, when the church understands the doctrine of sin, it will accept the fact that the only ministry to which it is called is this ministry of grace. To transmit the facts of the gospel story, to drill the student in the definitions of atonement, to define with clarity the nature of the Christian life—all of these are of no value if the heart has not been changed.

Therefore, the church may well curtail the strenuous program of activity by which it often tries to promote the Kingdom of God, and may well spend itself in bearing witness to God's grace. For as Calvin points out in *The Institutes,* a man cannot confess his sins and surrender his heart to God until he knows he has been forgiven.[10] Only then will the words and definitions of the church's creeds make sense.

Like Jesus Christ, whose body it is, the church faces two ways—toward God and toward man. Identifying itself with all mankind in its sin, it looks to God for forgiveness and redemption. Having been forgiven and brought into new life through God's grace, it becomes the instrument of his grace and looks to man in compassion and love.

The church performs its ministry of grace in two ways: by telling its story of God's grace, and by reflecting toward other persons the grace the church has itself known.

The first of these has reference to the unity and simplicity of the church's message. The church knows nothing but that it has been forgiven. The Bible's one story is a story of how this came about. It is a story that bears telling again and again. The world may grow weary of church suppers and bazaars, but it never grows weary of hearing that God yearns over man and spends himself in seeking companionship with man. Children may be taught the geography of Palestine—and indeed should be taught it in order that the incarnation of God in Jesus Christ may become to them a real incarnation occurring at a time and place—but it will be the grace of God shining through the face of Christ and not the geography of Palestine that will set boys and girls free to love the right and try to follow it.

The second way in which the church performs its ministry of grace is by reflecting the grace it has known in Christ Jesus. Grace once become incarnate in Jesus Christ must continue incarnate in his church. God found man unable to respond to grace—indeed, unable to recognize it in its fullness and beauty—until he could see it in another man, until he could experience it face to face in a relationship with a man. The church was born when the disciples began to recognize what had happened to them in Jesus Christ. The church spread through the Mediterranean and then through the world when the world began to discover in the church the same kind of grace that the church had known in Christ. This is our mission—having been able to deal with our own sins by his grace, to reflect that grace so that others may be able to deal with their sins.

Sin can be dealt with only where both righteousness and forgiving love are known. To display or to require righteousness
without love only aggravates the predicament, driving the other
to despair. To show forgiving love without any standard of right
only intensifies the guilt and engulfs the other in an intolerable
freedom. A wise teacher or parent who has known both righteousness and forgiveness is able in some measure to offer a grace in
which another can acknowledge his predicament and need of forgiveness, and is able to establish limits within which another can
learn to deal with his own life.

This is the most costly aspect of the church's ministry. It requires the teacher to have the deep regard and respect for the
learner that will enable him to struggle with his sin in his own
way and at his own speed. It requires teachers to understand the
stages or levels through which personality develops, the deviations
from the norm that are likely to occur, the particular kind of
need that may be reflected in the deviation. It requires that the
greedy, selfish child who repels rather than attracting be sur-
rounded with particular affection in order that the deep hunger
that expresses itself in greed may be filled. It requires that the
dominating elder in the church be recognized as one who has
himself been dominated and who will go on bearing the sins of
the fathers until the grace reflected in the church can set him
free. It requires that the gossipy woman be given a taste of the real
communion for which God created her so that she may be lifted
out of her pettiness and taught to express grace herself.

The cost of grace is confession of one's own sin and willingness
to bear with Christ the sins of the other. Both are required if the
church is to perform its mission.

The biblical doctrine of man calls for a leadership that believes
in the priesthood of all believers, all men serving as priests to one
another. It forbids all leaders in the church to be jealous of their
roles as leader. It asks of them a willingness to let others step in
where they themselves cannot lead, a willingness to participate
in a fellowship they do not dominate. The awareness that all
are sinners falling short of the glory of God, and that all who are

redeemed are now ministers of his grace, gives humility and generosity with regard to leadership.

This was one of the last lessons the disciples learned. On the very road to the cross they quarreled about their relative importance in the Kingdom, jealous for the right to rule, not seeing yet what love of Christ requires. Freedom from the covetousness of position is freedom to teach—to point to truth, to open new windows to the soul, to suggest new paths—with no attempt to restrain the one who looks out these windows and ventures down these paths, with no attempt to cover up the hesitation in one's self that holds one back from discovery. The church's educational ministry must be of this sort. Dietrich Bonhoffer says: "It is hard for the sated and the mighty to grasp the meaning of God's judgement and God's mercy. . . . it is hard to attain to the simplicity of the surrender of the heart to Jesus Christ."[11]

The Church's Responsibility to Trust in the Reality of New Life

The fourth implication of the Christian doctrine of man is that the church must have the courage to take seriously its hope of new life. One suspects that the reason for the church's habit of ignoring the doctrine of sin is its lack of faith in the reality of redemption. The church refuses to face man's tragic predicament and defines sin in superficial moralistic and legalistic terms because it can see a way to tackle the job on that level. It can compel people to conform to convention. But it does not really have confidence in the miracle of the new birth. Revolutions are frightening to little minds. Like the woman who refused to eat okra, most of us do not want anything we cannot control. The church has always in one way or another tried to shackle its saints and prophets in their lifetime because they reveal a power the church cannot account for on its own terms.

The biblical doctrine of man requires the church to have the courage to believe in the promise of redemption. A teacher or preacher in the church—and all of us are teachers and preachers— must have a profound optimism about the persons entrusted to his care, that they can be changed and that they want to be.

Indications of indifference to the gospel are attempts to cover up the real yearning that is there. Only the Pharisees among us, who have persuaded themselves that no change is required, are actually indifferent to a word of Good News. All others—the withdrawn, the aggressive, the dependent—yearn to be free of themselves. No one wants to be bound by despair. Everyone wants to be at peace with God and man, and signs that point to the contrary are themselves cries for help.

Thus we may take heart even when the teen-ager gives every appearance of sheer defiance, or the woman down the street turns away in what appears to be indifference. God has given himself from the beginning of the world to the redemption of men and we can take heart that more than anything else in the world he wants these in his family and counts them his own even when they spurn his advances. The church can do no less in his name. Our acceptance of justification at the hands of God requires us to "justify" our brother when he stands before us caught in his own evil-doing. Our ministry to him is an extension to him of what measure of God's grace we can reflect in our lives—in the hope that he may through the church be pointed to God.

This is not to say that God has entrusted to the church the forgiveness of sins. This is God's prerogative and his only. No one of us is fit to bind and loose the sins of another. But he has charged us with the necessity of announcing to the world that the world is forgiven and of bearing in ourselves the image of his grace, of living among men as those who know the gift of redemption for themselves and who thereby point always to the assurance of God's grace for all others.

The assurance that we have ourselves been forgiven gives us assurance that this other may have hope; it sends us back to try once more to break through the wall that has been thrown around this self. It makes the teacher—who has had a profound sense of his own sin and who recalls the deep, almost hopeless longing that once filled his heart—know that there is no point at which he can say, "I have done enough." The memory of the persistent love of God that would not quit, no matter what, drives him back once more.

"Working together with him then, we entreat you not to accept the grace of God in vain." (2 Corinthians 6:1)

CHAPTER THREE

We Are All Barabbas

One of the most difficult problems faced by the church is the problem of teaching Christian ethics. If we could accept an intellectualistic and legalistic view of our faith, it would be easy enough to transmit to the people of every generation the creeds and catechism for their faith, and the laws and precepts for their life, and to discover sanctions by which we could insure a relative conformity to church convention. If we could accept the perfectionist view of man we could at least try—as we have been doing—to establish some progressive standard and assist persons to measure up to that standard at each stage of life. But a life of forgiveness and hope requires another approach altogether and sends the church to its knees to acknowledge its unsuitability for the task. In this very acknowledgment—or confession—lies the church's hope.

THE STORY OF BARABBAS, OUR STARTING POINT

The Nobel prize-winning novel entitled *Barabbas*,[1] written in 1951 by Pär Lagerkvist, is a dramatic and penetrating portrayal of the church's responsibility for the salvation of the world and

71

the church's inadequacy for the task in and of itself. This novel, therefore, might well serve as the starting point for this consideration of the Protestant ethic.

The story begins with Barabbas, the one for whom Christ died, set free at the last moment before his death and sent back to the world to live the life he owed another man. As you can imagine, the event set up a strange turmoil within him. Why do I say "as you can imagine"? I should say "as you know," for this same experience that happened to Barabbas has happened to us all. Christ died in his stead no more truly than he died in ours.

As Lagerkvist tells the story, Barabbas never really found the Christ, who had so changed the course of his life; and although throughout the rest of his days he was drawn irresistibly toward the early church, he could never find his way into the fellowship of the church. Moreover, the early Christians could never quite accept Barabbas as one of them, but held him apart with a strange horror as though he alone had been the cause of Christ's death.

The novel is a haunting story. The portrait of the church that turned away from Barabbas is a portrait of ourselves, as the portrait of Barabbas is a portrait of ourselves. For we are all Barabbas— the man for whom Christ died, the acquitted one. And we are also the church that turned away from him.

It is the very heart of the gospel that Christ died for us that we might live for him. It is the meaning of the church that we are to extend grace to the other that he may be able to live as a follower of Christ. In this story, the Swedish novelist has spelled out a parable of the church's responsibility to mediate grace to all the men for whom Christ died and the impossibility of doing that unless we know that we are also Barabbas.

The question with which this chapter deals is "What is the church's task in Christian ethics?" If the tendency in the church to resort to moralism and legalism, teaching moral axioms as if man can become good simply by deciding to do so, is foreign to the true nature of the church, then how can we describe the task in accordance with the real meaning of the gospel? What must the church do to lead men into the new life?

Let me suggest the twofold nature of this task:

(1) First, to enable a man to come to Christ so that he may be set free of his old pattern of life and thought, and may live as befits a follower of Christ. If it be true that a man cannot do the right simply because he knows the right but must be changed at his heart so that he is empowered for the right, then clearly the first and major task of the church has to do with the church's responsibility as ambassador of God's grace. For it is by grace that a man is first forgiven and then transformed and created anew.

Dr. Paul Scherer says Christian ethics is faith gone on an errand. If so, the church must proclaim the Good News which elicits faith in a man, so that he may then begin to act as a man of faith.

(2) Second, to assist its people to know what the Christian faith requires in this situation in which God has placed them, and to give them the courage to do it.

Before we can describe with any exactness this twofold task of the church, however, it is necessary to examine the nature of Christian ethics—that is, the nature of forgiveness and the nature of freedom.

THE ETHICS OF THE NEW COVENANT—THE ETHICS OF FORGIVENESS AND FREEDOM

The life of the follower of Jesus Christ can best be described as the life of the forgiven one—or to use the language of the courtroom in keeping with the doctrine of justification by faith, the acquitted one. Christian behavior is a particular kind of behavior that is not possible for a man until he has become a Christian. He cannot by simply deciding to do so start living a life of fellowship with God and man and find the inner peace for which he longs. Before he is set free for fellowship and communion a great new experience must befall him—an experience of such proportions that he knows himself to be in a different estate.

This is what forgiveness is—an experience of being removed from one estate to another, from the estate of outcast who cannot love to the estate of adopted one. The new estate is the awareness of having been chosen, elected for a place in a family to which one has no claim.

When forgiveness is seen in the total biblical context it means, as we have seen, inclusion in covenant. When we seek to discover the nature of Christian ethics, we find it to be the ethics of the New Covenant, or the ethics of forgiveness and freedom. When one has known the experience of adoption, he can begin to act like the family into which he has been adopted.

The Releasing and Transforming Power of Forgiveness

Forgiveness is not an isolated fragment of the Christian gospel but the very heart of it. It implies a completely new kind of relationship between persons. It is restoration to community. Forgiveness is the mark of God's outreach to man, by which God seeks to overcome man's inability to enter into fellowship. Forgiveness is the clearest expression we have of God's way of acting in history, his yearning for community no matter what. Forgiveness is God's way of reaching through the hostility by which man seeks to protect himself to the hungering heart of man.

There is only one source from which forgiveness may come: that is the utterly righteous love of God himself. God in his infinite wisdom and in his infinite righteousness is willing to extend love in order that man may be set free to enter into fellowship with God, where he can be filled with God's righteousness.

Forgiveness rests upon the sovereignty of God's grace, the aseity of God. It has its source in the Loving One who, needing nothing for himself, wants fellowship with man at whatever cost. Forgiveness is the gift of the sovereign Lord of all life, whose compassion and love lead him into fellowship or community with those who are in no measure ready for fellowship, in order that they may be

made ready. "We are elected into love," says the countess in
Christopher Fry's play, *The Dark Is Light Enough*. We see it at
the Exodus, when God extends his hand to a people who are
"no people" to make them his people. We see it in Hosea, where
the prophet explains God's capacity to forgive and go on loving
as resting simply in the fact that he is God.

"How can I give you up, O Ephraim! . . .
I will not execute my fierce anger . . .
for I am God and not man,
the Holy One in your midst."[2]

This is the fact that sets Christianity apart from all other
religions the world has known, this dimension of pure, uncalculat-
ing love. God comes to man saying, "I love you. I want you for
my people." He bridges the gulf between God and man as though
there were no gulf—for there is no gulf when love takes hold.
The love of God for man, like human sin, which is the opposite
of love, refuses to yield to logic. It makes no sense by any human
standard. Explain it as you like, there is a leftover, an irreducible
factor, a surd. "I am God and not man. I will not let you go."
"The promise of God," says Calvin, "is, I shall make them to
love me."

But forgiveness may be mediated through persons who know
themselves to be forgiven, who, as Paul Tillich puts it, are "transparent" to the grace of God. Forgiveness may also be the act of
one whose own status has been miraculously changed by the
forgiveness of God. A man, freely and graciously forgiven his own
most heinous sin, is by that act of forgiveness moved out of the
whole calculating way of life to live in community where grace
and not calculus rules. "United with him in a death like his, we
shall certainly be united with him in a resurrection like his."[3]

The same quality of grace that marks God may in some
measure—must in some measure—mark the man who has been
recipient of such grace. An utterly new quality comes into his life.
Captured by the absurdity of his position, he sees the absurdity
of calculation. He is set free from man's insatiable yearning to
control—set free to love. He moves over into a whole new way

of looking at life—the way of grace. Such a one is not given the power of forgiving another his sins. Only God can forgive sin. But a forgiven one can forgive what another has done to him, and show grace to another, thus revealing to him the possibility of ultimate forgiveness; and then he can point to the source of forgiveness.

The word "covenant" is associated in the Bible with this relationship of God to man that is established when man has been forgiven. "Covenant" is normally a bargaining word. The human race has no other words than bargaining words until God breaks through. For the unregenerate life is a bargaining life. When God breaks through into his life, however, man's very vocabulary is transformed, and he has a new orientation to life. Then he is able to take a familiar word from our "marketing orientation" and fill it full of new meaning. Agape is a case in point. I am told it was a little-used word, humble, insignificant, when taken over into the context of faith. But when used to describe God's love, it introduced a whole new dimension into human thought. Covenant is another such word.

When the word "covenant" is coupled with grace, it becomes a covenant as unlike a human contract as agape is unlike Hollywood. It is a pledge of God's eternal faithfulness to man, a guarantee of security no matter what. It asks faithfulness of man and gives a picture of what faithfulness is like. By that very picture it shows that faithfulness is unconditional. Faithfulness does not depend upon external circumstances, but upon the character of the one who covenants. God's pledge to man depends on the strength of God and is directed toward the weakness of man. "I am your God," he says, "I will go on being your God. Nothing you will do can change that."

On this basis of covenant man can live, knowing that the future will be as the past has been—that God, who has manifested himself as Lover, will go on loving. Within such assurance of love man dares to acknowledge his sin. He is able to face himself as he is, knowing that even such a one as he will not be rebuffed. God is willing to be his God. Calvin points out in *The Institutes* that a man cannot truly devote himself to repentance unless he knows himself to be of God.[4]

Forgiveness and covenant are correlatives. If sin is inability to love, inability to enter into community, forgiveness is extension of community into which one may enter. Forgiveness is invitation to community on the only terms on which man can enter—that is, assurance that community will not be withdrawn. This is the meaning of covenant and the meaning of justification by faith— a guarantee of continuing love no matter what.

The incapacity of man to repent of his sins and enter into covenant before he knows forgiveness beyond the shadow of any doubt is the condition that requires the Messiah. Jeremiah foresaw a day when God would break through into the heart of man with his forgiving love, enabling man to enter into community with God and man as he had never been able to do. This was the work of Christ. Christ is the revelation of God's approachability, an expression of God's gracious, forgiving love as God approaches man. But more than that, Christ was the love of God itself that extended God's forgiveness to men and caught men up into a fellowship that transformed their hearts.

The deeper dimension of the New Covenant, which is made with sinful man at what great cost to God, was not made known to man merely in what Christ said of God, but also and primarily in what he did in the name of God. The real meaning of forgiveness was known only after the death and resurrection of Christ. Then the disciples were able to see that the death of Jesus Christ was their death. Then were they able to interpret its meaning in terms of forgiveness. With the death and resurrection of Christ, the disciples could face the fact of their own sin, acknowledging its gravity. For at the same time they could accept the fact that God loved so much that he would identify himself with sinful man—would become sin for and with man. Then they were able to enter into covenant with God in the only way a sinful man can enter covenant with a righteous God.

This is faith as it is intended in the biblical doctrine of justifi-

cation by faith—to come to God with a new heart, a heart into
which the Spirit of God has entered, a heart made new by
identification with Christ.

Faith is acceptance of the full revelation of God in Jesus Christ
and entrance into fellowship with him on those terms. It is
acceptance of God's grace—which is acceptance of one's own sin;
acceptance of God's grace—which is acceptance of his forgiveness
and of the freedom to live in the family like a son.

It was this that never happened to Barabbas in his lifetime,
as Lagerkvist tells it. He never knew the meaning of the grace
that resulted in his acquittal. He was constrained by the man who
died on his cross. He could never get free of him. But he had no
other acquaintance with grace. Barabbas was unable to surrender
himself to anyone, and so was unable to surrender to Christ. Forgiveness means not simply acquittal, wiping out the offense, but reconciliation or restoration to fellowship. To accept forgiveness
is to be set free of guilt as well as condemnation and to enter
community.

Lagerkvist tells us that Barabbas had no acquaintance with
grace such as would convince him of its reality. He had been
born in hatred; he wore a deep scar on his face, put there by his
father, whom he had then killed. He had known love of a kind—
love of his peers, his fellow slaves. But he had no experience in
which he might deal with his own sin in the presence of one
whom he had offended and who now forgives. Grace and forgiveness are empty words unless one has known the reality of grace
and forgiveness in one's own life, mediated through the relationship of those who have themselves faced their own sin and accepted God's grace.

This is the first part of the Christian ethic—accepting forgiveness for one's self and announcing the availability of forgiveness
for all mankind. It will be well to look now at the second aspect
of the ethics of the New Covenant—the nature of the life of faith.
What is it like to be a member of the New Covenant having been
brought there through God's forgiveness in Christ?

Freedom in the Life of the New Covenant

Life in the New Covenant is a life of freedom. One who is forgiven is set free of condemnation and guilt, set free to live in covenant with God and man.

"Freedom" is a word of great ambiguity in Christian theology, but a word essential in the description of the covenant life. We cannot give it up even though it is often misleading; we must instead clarify it for greater use. The acceptance of forgiveness sets a man free so that he can begin to live the covenant life. He is free from guilt so that he can look another in the face without shrinking back, free from shame so that he can move out toward every man with head erect, free from covetousness so that he can give to another without thereby giving up the structure of his life and the root of security, free from the necessity to resist and attack and dominate.

The acceptance of forgiveness sets a man free *to* as well as free *from*. It sets him free to absorb hostility instead of resisting it, free to forgive evil instead of returning it, free to trust another instead of suspecting, free to serve instead of being served. This is the mark of the man who lives under the ethics of justification by faith.

But such freedom is always a bondage to God, and this is man's hope. Man is not a self-sufficient being. As creature he does not contain the absolutes within himself. His freedom does not mean liberty to do what he pleases. It means freedom to do what God pleases. Freedom in Christ is not undirected liberty. It is covenant with God in Christ, bondage to God. This is the hidden meaning of justification by faith. Faith takes a man into the household of God where he is strengthened and supported by the Father. Faith surrounds him with the "saints" who, like himself, are seeking the Father's will. Faith identifies him with the Christ, as Paul's phrase "in Christ" suggests. Faith opens his heart to the indwelling of the Spirit of God so that his life may begin to reflect the image of God.

This is man's hope—not that he is made perfect but that he is set free from fear and brought into the presence of God.

THE CHURCH'S TASK IN CHRISTIAN ETHICS

Having described the nature of Christian ethics as the ethics of forgiveness and freedom, we can come now to the specific question that concerns us: What is the church's part in leading men into this new life of forgiveness and freedom? How can the church through its educational program open to its members the possibility of this new quality of life, thus setting them free of the necessity to justify themselves before God and man? What is the church's part in freeing its people of the calculating legalistic goodness that so often besets church people, so that they may glorify God and enjoy him?

Let me mention three aspects of the church's task in this matter: first, to make known the fact of the New Covenant, drawing men into the covenant, through which they may be set free; second, to support men in their new-found freedom while they struggle to find God's way; and third, to teach the nature of the new life in covenant with God.

Drawing Men Into the New Covenant

It has been said repeatedly in these chapters that it is the function of the church to be both witness and instrument of God's revelation of himself to man. Now let it be said specifically that the church is witness and instrument of the New Covenant God has made with man in Jesus Christ. As Israel was created for the glory of God, to witness to God through its covenant life with him, and to serve as instrument through which all the peoples of the world would be blessed, so the church is created to draw men into the New Covenant in Christ Jesus. Its primary task with relation to Christian ethics is that of pointing to the New Covenant in which man is set free to love.

The church's first way of pointing to the New Covenant is to proclaim the story of God's action in history as it is narrated in Scripture, in which God has made his grace known to men in Jesus Christ. This is the best way in which the church can help men to know God as he wishes to be known, for the event of Jesus Christ is the only event in which God's fullness has been made plain.

The church must tell the story with humble pride and profound love as the story of its Lord and of its life. Its purpose in telling is that the listener may come to know the Christ as the church knows him and may also enter into covenant with him. The church must stand beside the Christ it speaks of, inviting the listener into fellowship. It must stand beside the listener looking toward the Christ for life, trusting in him as the means of access to God.

The church tends to forget the particular function of the Scriptures in God's redemptive plan, however, and often uses the Scripture to augment man's plight instead of to release man from his plight. It draws on the Bible for moralisms the people cannot bear because of their sin, for examples of piety the people cannot follow. The Bible is not a book of morals but a witness to God's grace and forgiveness. It records events in the history of the Hebrews which under the influence of the Holy Spirit they were able to interpret as acts of God for man's salvation; and it records the event of Jesus Christ in which God's forgiveness is fully realized. The Bible story is the story of God's grace for all men and an invitation to covenant. The words of life it speaks are words of proclamation and invitation. It is a proclamation of God's grace, and an invitation to accept God's grace as the foundation and God himself as the center of one's own life. It is not written to tell us how to behave except in a secondary sense, for man cannot behave like a Christian unless he has the Spirit of Christ in him. It is not written to solve man's problems, nor to give man peace of mind, for peace of mind comes only through Jesus Christ. Eventually the Bible does all of these things. The Bible was written because God had something to say to man, and because man, in listening to God's words, has found a way to life with God. It contains the single story of God's acts of redemption for man—a story which in the very telling of it brings life to the listener.

To know that it is wrong to steal will not keep me from stealing. Most thieves would acknowledge the evil of their behavior. To know that Abraham was a man of faith and that he was blessed will not strengthen my faith. But to know that God loves me so much and wants me to be his so much that he would in Jesus Christ become sin for me—this love of Christ constrains me.

In order to point to the New Covenant the church must not only tell the story of its life but must itself stand before the world as the repentant and forgiven community. It may not stand apart from the world as better than the world, for pride repels men rather than drawing them. The church must stand within the world as a people who know where grace is found. The church must bear witness to God not only by proclaiming the story, but by becoming a listening, repenting community, coming together again and again to listen to the story of its own life—how God before the foundation of the world destined it to be his people, how God has worked throughout human history to create a people with whom he can live, setting man free by his atoning act in Christ, and calling him into his household.

Thus the church itself is to be marked by freedom—freedom from guilt, from shame; freedom from the law, and thus freedom to love; freedom from the bondage of the customary and traditional, and thus freedom for adventure and for discovery of new meaning; freedom from fear and from greed, and thus freedom to attack exploitation and injustice wherever they may be found.

Moreover, the church must stand as witness in its own *koinonia* —"the costly fruit of God's self-offering." The church is to be bound together in one body—members, as Calvin put it, "of his own Son Jesus." "Behold," the New Testament world said, "behold, how these Christians love one another."

Moreover, the church points to the New Covenant by extending covenant to its fellow men. As was pointed out in chapter two, the church is steward of God's grace—those to whom grace has been extended and through whom it is to be administered. The church is God's instrument through which the reality of grace is not merely to be talked about but through which it can be made known. In this body, and in this body only, grace becomes incarnate, for where God's grace is known, there is the church.

When the Christian church, knowing itself to be forgiven because of God's grace, is able to extend grace to another, it is the church. When it is able, as Christ was able, to reach out to sinful men and women without condemnation, extending to them the warmth of love and trust, the church is the steward of God's grace. Then does the word of acquittal take on meaning and bear fruit in reconciliation and a life of fidelity and love. Love, which the law demands, has no regard for anybody's merit, and pours itself alike upon the unworthy, the wicked, and those without gratitude."[5]

The church is under obligation to reflect in its own life this same grace which it has known in Christ Jesus and to proclaim this grace in its preaching and teaching. If the church is to serve as God's instrument it is essential that it reveal in its life the meaning of grace and the nature of fruits of the spirit, that it embody grace and thus make it real in the experience of others, representing to man the nature of God's love for him.

The reflection of grace in the life of the church, however, is and has to be spontaneous and uncalculated. It is simply an unconscious reflection in its own life of the deep experiences it has undergone. It cannot be contrived for the purpose of teaching without thereby becoming hypocrisy, in which case it is obviously self-defeating. This aspect of the teaching process can be discerned by another; it can even be pointed out by another; but it never can be included in a planned program of education. Nevertheless, there are several significant and indispensable elements in this spontaneous teaching of the church to which attention can be called and to which the church can give itself: repentence and acceptance of forgiveness; identification with Barabbas, whoever he be; inclusion of Barabbas in the community of worship and fellowship; freedom in Christ to express one's faith without apology, as one is able; acknowledgment of the freedom of the other to live also as one forgiven and free.

It was the tragedy of Barabbas that in this terrible instance the church was unable to serve as Christ's instrument, that the church was not "transparent" to God's grace, as so often since it has not been transparent to God's grace. This is the eternal humiliation of the church, that it fails to represent the eternal Son of God, who would comfort and support the sin-sick world. And so Barabbas was denied the one thing which might have had the power to transform his heart—the enfolding love of those who could identify themselves with him. His disturbing glimpse of Jesus had left him forever discontented with life as he had known it, forever yearning for the fellowship he saw in the church and was not permitted to enter. This is the terrifying truth that describes the real function of the church—the truth that until men know love in the flesh, feeling its arms about them, they cannot know God. Grace is the mark of the church. Those who have not known the reality of grace may in the name of Christ help Nero set fire to Rome as Lagerkvist pictures Barabbas doing. They may, like Barabbas, go on through life seeing the world as an odious world to be destroyed rather than a beloved world to be saved.

It is somewhere here that the clue to the tragic situation in the South today can be found. The bitterness, the twisted concept of man, the arrogance and prejudice that would destroy a whole system of education rather than acknowledge the common brotherhood of man—rather than sit down beside another man to read.

Grace, as made known in Jesus Christ, is identification with all men. It is made possible for the church only when it knows that the church, like Barabbas, is also acquitted by the death of Christ, and that there is no real difference between one reprieved sinner and another.

The church's one goal in its educational work, as throughout its whole mission, is to present the gospel message of God's grace in such a way that a person who receives it can make real decisions about it. This is all the church can do—except to crush human selves when it undertakes something outside its jurisdiction. It cannot legislate for the new life. It cannot transform persons. It cannot require conformity to a pattern. The church can serve as God's instrument only by going to the world with the story of God's truth and God's grace—the truth about God which tears down and builds up—and a life of grace which bears witness to this same truth.

Supporting Men in the Freedom of the New Covenant

The church is not only witness and instrument of the New Covenant, created by God to point to his grace and to mediate his grace to the world in order that men may be set free; the church must also support its people in their freedom and teach its people the meaning of the New Covenant and its way of life.

To support a people newly born into Christ is no easy task, and the church has all too often failed to recognize its difficulty. It is true that the church has tried to teach for Christian behavior. Indeed, much of its preaching and teaching has been largely moral or ethical in intent. But, as has been pointed out, the church, in failing to recognize the nature of Christian ethics, has failed to take account of the real problem of the covenant life—the peril of freedom and the requirements of love.

The church in its educational program has tended to forget both its function as steward of God's grace and the limitations this puts upon its work. Its function as steward of grace arises from the fact that it has itself been the recipient of God's grace. The limitations put upon its work stem from the church's doctrine of man. This doctrine, as we have seen, holds that man is a person responsible to act for himself but unable to act for himself unless he is surrendered to God and willing to accept God's righteousness as the standard of his life. Such surrender is an inner act of the soul made possible by a prior act upon him which he recognizes and responds to with his whole heart. "True keeping of the law grows out of love which is offered freely."[6]

When such an act has taken place, the newborn soul can begin to structure his life around its new center. Then it must struggle to conform to the new pattern. The struggle is not an easy one, and the struggling one will waver back and forth, now meeting his mark, now falling flat on his face. To all external appearances there has been no change from the wayward one who also used to miss as often as he made the proper gestures. Only those who are taken into his confidence can know that he is turned now in another direction and that his movements, though apparently the same, have a completely different meaning.

But the church, overlooking this fact about man's freedom, often turns its attention to the external act alone and assumes a responsibility that is untrue to its own nature and to the nature of man. Then it scolds its people for their sins and exhorts them to righteousness, forgetting that to know the right does not give a man the power to do it, but only intensifies his distress and guilt without giving him a way out; forgetting that the church is summoned not to redo man according to its own desires, but to manifest the grace of its Lord by means of which man may be made whole. James Smart says that this moralism of the church "fails to take account of how deep the roots of conduct are, and that disorder in conduct usually has beneath it, not just an ignorance of what is right, but a disorder in the self that renders it incapable of right action."[7]

In its educational program the church must in every way take full account of this need for deep inner change and for a matrix of grace within which the new life may be fostered. It must know clearly what its business is as church, how far its powers go, at what points it has no function to perform. The church has not thought clearly about itself in these respects, and needs to give careful attention to setting its objectives with these matters in mind.

The church's one objective is so to present Christ that the individual may respond to him. More specific goals for the individual must be set by the individual himself when he has been taken hold of by God's grace and begins to have hope of new life. The teacher's own goals may be expressed in terms of what he himself hopes to do in his teaching—how he will tell the story of God's love, how he will meet the pupil's need, how he will express his own faith. The goals for the pupil must be set by the pupil when he catches a vision of the possibility that lies before him. What he needs from the church is a matrix of grace within which he can bear the agony of change.

It has been said repeatedly here that the Christian life is the outcome of the Christian faith. Paul calls it the "fruit of the Spirit," the visible expression of the Spirit of Christ dwelling in the heart of the believer.

Paul's phrase "in Christ"—which Deissmann says occurs 159 times in Paul's letters—points to the personal identification of Christ with man, of man with Christ, that expresses itself in the kind of covenant living we find described in the New Testament. This is clearly no artificial conformity, no enforced legalism, but the fruit of a relationship to God made possible by God's gift of forgiveness and man's response of faith.

Although fruit, however, Christian behavior is not involuntary, and the church as witness and instrument of God's revelation has a function to perform here which it dare not neglect. Fruit of the Spirit is different from the fruit of a tree. Fruit of the Spirit is an act of will and purpose—purpose to do the will of God, whose Spirit it is. It is a matter of decision, often difficult Gethsemane decision, decision to die if need be for the accomplishment of one's purpose.

Let no one assume that it is easy for a Christian to make a decision. Christian decisions are no mechanical matter. There is no blueprint for decisions at any point. The man of faith must act in faith. It is true that there is a law of God which was given in clear and forthright words for the direction of frail humanity. But this very law, when taken as the ultimate, became man's death instead of his life. Only the man who knows Christ can take the law as his guide without being crushed by it. Calvin says, "A sincere love of the law of God is a sure sign of our adoption because it is a work of the Spirit."[8] But the price of justification by faith is freedom from the minutiae of the law. This is a terrible freedom that leaves man with the obligation to make his own decisions in the love of Christ at every point. Dostoievsky's Grand Inquisitor was right when he said to Jesus, "Nothing has ever been more insupportable for a man and a human society than freedom."[9] But he was wrong when he said it was the job of the church to relieve man of this freedom.

The church is under obligation to help its people know what to do with the freedom given it in Christ. Freedom is a tightrope between moralism on the one hand and relativism or antinomianism on the other; and mankind cannot keep his balance without the support of the church. There are many signs that young people today—indeed, that most people—are afraid of freedom. They are cautious, wanting to be sure before acting. Like Gideon they want a sign. But the church cannot give a sign that has not already been given by God in Jesus Christ. Freedom without grace would be unmanageable indeed. And the church must provide for its people and for the world the atmosphere of grace within which a man may have the courage to make an honest decision and move toward the likeness of Jesus Christ.

Justification by faith means that salvation does not depend on a man's goodness. It means, moreover, that God does not remove his presence or take away his love when a man makes a wrong decision. This fact sets a man free to decide bravely even at the risk of deciding wrongly. He is relieved of the "morbid preoccupation with his own moral balance sheet."[10] He is free to take his stand without regard for what he looks like to another. As I look at Christ I am impressed by his utter disregard for what men thought about his behavior. He had the invincible courage that came of knowing he belonged to God.

So the church must provide for its people the context of grace in which they can have the courage to make decisions and so can choose freely to act from the Father's love without fear of losing the church's support—for this is man's hope. The fruits of the Spirit are whatever actions of man are done freely—without coercion—because one knows the Father.

Joseph Sittler in *The Structure of Christian Ethics* puts it this way: "Christian ethics is the actualization of justification. For justification, being certified or made righteous in the God-relationship, bestows positive liberation to serve. This liberation exists inwardly because, as Luther puts it, 'God has taken care of my salvation in Christ,' and I am henceforth free as before God. This liberation exists outwardly because the energies which men futilely devote to the pleasing of God are now called out and exercised where God's purposes and family require them. When the self is known, loved, forgiven, then the self is set free in disciplined service to the will of God."[11]

The awareness of this function of the church and of the limits and the possibilities that press upon the church as it tries to teach Christian ethics to its people will enable the church to draw upon the data of all the man sciences without being betrayed into adopting the humanistic philosophy which often underlies the man sciences. The church can make full use of what psychology tells of the needs of persons at various levels of development, of the "developmental tasks" that they must undertake and the hazards they are likely to meet, of the symptoms of deep emotional disturbances that may offer a clue to the inner state of the soul. These psychological data will not set the church's goals for it; the church's goals are set by the gospel message itself. But these data will enable the church to undertake its task with greater clarity, preparing its literature, educating its teachers and parents in the light of the reticence and concern with which the church must always approach human nature.

The church has often in the past let psychology instead of the gospel determine its procedures. Having discovered what is the average for persons of various ages according to its statistical studies, it has assumed that the average is also the norm, and has attempted to hold this norm over the heads of teachers and parents alike, urging them to bend all their efforts to bring their charges to this point, making them nervous when the children for whom they are responsible do not measure up to this standard. Awareness of the church's limited responsibility in shaping the life of the child brings a new perspective, and with it a new enthusiasm in teaching.

It is God who changes human lives. The church can only point to God and surround with God's grace. This the church does best by its own faith in God, by its response to him of worship and work, by its deep concern for the persons whom God has made and whom he now calls to be his. Psychological data can assist the church to understand the struggles persons must go through in becoming what God has wanted them to become (the pain encountered when blocks have been set in their way by the world and by the church when the church is unfaithful). To know, for example, that a two-year-old—and a seventeen-year-old—is bound to say "no" for a time in order that he may learn to say "yes" with meaning, to know that this does not mean that parent or teacher is an abject failure, is a boundless comfort and enables the church to move forward in its program of nurture with confidence.

It is the responsibility of the church to support those whom Christ has set free in order that they may learn how to handle their freedom. This responsibility is not diminished by the fact that, being human, these new creations will make mistakes over and over again. This fact simply intensifies the task, calling for a fuller measure of grace on the part of those who have themselves known the grace of God.

Teaching the Nature of Life in the New Covenant

But it is not enough to point to God's act of grace in Jesus Christ and provide a matrix of grace in which the newborn soul may grow and struggle. The church must also help its people to know what it means to act in the Father's love.

Joseph Sittler goes on to say: "And this will of God is now confronted both as a known and as an unknown. It is known in Christ who is the incarnate concretion of God's ultimate and relentless will-to-restoration; and it remains unknown in the fact that the actual service of this will is presented to the believer not as a general program given in advance but as an ever-changing and fluctuant obligation to the neighbor in the midst of history's life."[12]

Here again the figures of the covenant with God and the household of God stand us in good stead. Biblical ethics are covenant ethics, the ethics of the household, justification ethics.[13] The Christian faith offers man another set of mores which may be called the mores of the Kingdom of God.[14] Simply put—too simply—we say the Christian ethic is an ethic of love. Paul Ramsey in his book *Basic Christian Ethics*[15] says it is nothing but an ethic of love. Nothing is required of the Christian except what love requires. Everything is required of the Christian which love requires.

Thus Alexander Miller can describe Christian ethics by saying that it "differs from idealist ethics in that its absolute is an absolute loyalty and not an absolute principle." There is in the Christian ethic both "an absolute element and an element of calculation."[16] The absolute is the freedom to love and the requirement to love. The calculation is the calculation of love's demands at any particular point.

The calculation of what love requires at any point must take into account the need of the beloved, and the resources of the lover. It is never the same in any two situations. This is why the law always falls short. The law prescribes precisely the action to be performed without regard to circumstances. What love requires is to be arrived at only by the most scrupulous attention to the needs of the beloved.

In situations where this relationship is purely personal and individual, the relation simply of one person to another person, the beloved's need can be readily discerned, for love drives us to identification with the other, to stand where he stands. However, in situations where masses of people are involved and where love's task requires a consideration of political forces and economic power structures, love's requirements are more difficult to discern. An act which might have brought about reconciliation in the relatively simple agricultural society of colonial days will not do so in the complex industrial situations of the twentieth century. Television and airplanes have made us neighbors with the whole of mankind, as Calvin said we must be, but the gigantic corporations that have made television and airlines possible have made ordinary expressions of neighborliness irrelevant, and relevant expressions of neighborliness almost impossible.

When one employs a maid to clean the apartment, one can be sure one pays fair wages for a job done well. When one purchases a vacuum cleaner made and sold by a process that involves a whole society of persons in steel industry, in wood building, in cloth weaving, in electrical engineering, and whole teams of salesmen and accountants and stenographers, it is somewhat more difficult to fulfill one's responsibility to the brother.

In its use of the Bible in teaching the requirements of love, the church will find that the very nature of the Bible provides this same perspective on Christian behavior. The Bible tells the story of the love of God as it reaches out to man no matter what, and it describes the righteousness of God in unmistakable terms. Then it leaves man free to decide what he will do with this message.

The one story that threads its way through the whole offers the clue to the use of the Bible in teaching Christian ethics. The Bible may not be used except to tell this story. Every story which makes up the one story, every verse, must be understood in its relation to this. So the church is forbidden to choose its own message which it thinks the world needs to hear and to select a Bible story out of context to reinforce this teaching. The Bible stands in judgment on the church, not the church on the Bible. To use a Bible story for its "secondary meaning" rather than for its "primary meaning," then, is likely to distort the Bible message. To use the Bible as buttress for extrabiblical ideas out of harmony with the one message of the Bible is dishonest and quite likely to prove destructive. The gospel of God is designed to meet man's need, and no human substitute is likely to be one fraction as salutary.

Thus it is generally *safer*—although not always desirable—in teaching the requirements of the gospel for one's life to start from the Bible story and move to the story's relevance for life. This is not so likely to distort and mislead. However, it is often necessary to start from human need in order to get man to listen to the Bible at all. For man has been disappointed many times in the

church's interpretation—or should I not say "misinterpretation"?—
of the Bible, and has turned away in indifference. He has been
sorely tried by the buffetings of the world and, for the lack of
a healing word, has become desperate. In his indifference and des-
peration he cannot take his attention from himself until he is
assured that what he will hear carries a healing power. But when
one starts his teaching with man and goes to the Bible with a
question on his lips, he must do so with caution, remembering that
the Bible has its own questions to ask. It does not have to answer
the questions of another; it may instead pronounce a judgment
upon the question or require an answer of the other. But its
promise is that when one answers "yes" to the question the Bible
asks, all other questions can be eventually answered.

The "ethical teachings" of the New Testament as they are
generally thought of—that is, the Sermon on the Mount and
other sayings of our Lord, the ethical portions of Paul's letters,
etc.—are to be recognized as secondary to the gospel. These are
descriptions of the new life which has been given in Christ. They
are not to be taught as laws. They are affirmations. This does
not mean that they are any the less demanding; indeed, the
claim of Christ is a total claim. A person who has taken Christ as
his Lord will need now to give his careful attention to these ad-
monitions of Jesus to his disciples and of Paul to his flock so that
he may point his life sharply in the direction of Christ.

But God, in making man in his own image, has made him to
be a free person—that is, to act from his whole self rather than
to be pushed from without; and only that behavior that is freely
chosen because one knows God's love for him is behavior in response to God's act of grace. The teacher helps a person to stand
fast in his newly received freedom when he enables him to understand the alternatives and to choose the one to which he will
give himself with his whole heart.

One of the best ways yet discovered of teaching Christian ethics
is to lead students to read the Bible for the story it tells, identifying
themselves with the persons in both the Old and New Testaments
who have met God and have been forced to wrestle through the

issues thereby raised in their lives. The prophet's call is just such a call as comes to each of us as we live in a similarly pagan world. In the story of Moses, or Isaiah, or Jeremiah, the issues are lifted before us with compelling clarity if we go beyond the external circumstances to the confrontation of man with God which is there. The call of Christ to the Samaritan woman, or to the businessman Zacchaeus, or to Martha of Bethany, becomes Christ's call to us when we are permitted to participate in the event which confronted these.

The call of Christ is a personal call, a call to loyalty to Christ himself. It can be heard most forcibly when person is confronted by person, when an event that changed a life is made contemporary in our lives.

The church must hold before its people continually the strenuous ethic of the Suffering Servant and the needs of the world in which the body of the Servant is now placed. Justification by faith becomes an immorality if it does not continually send us out to discover afresh the relevance of the gospel to life, the meaning of the New Covenant of Christ's blood which was shed for all of us who are Barabbas.

"For he has made known to us in all wisdom and insight the mystery of his will, according to his purpose which he set forth in Christ as a plan for the fullness of time, to unite all things in him, things in heaven and things on earth." (Ephesians 1:9-10)

CHAPTER FOUR

The New Creation

The aspect of church life where there is the greatest skepticism today is the assumption that the church is a new creation of God. The world refuses to take seriously the miracle of the church. Moreover, the church itself refuses to take seriously its own miracle.

THE IMPORTANCE OF HISTORY TO THE CHURCH

The concern of these chapters is the concern that the church reflect in its life and work the full dimension of the Christian faith as set forth in the Bible and recaptured in the Protestant Reformation in the phrase "justification by faith." This concern has been expressed in the preceding chapters as concern for the church's heritage at three points:

First, its epistemology. The church's program of worship and work must take into account the reality of revelation and response —the certainty that God has revealed himself to man as one who loves man and wishes to live in covenant with man; the certainty that man may respond to God in faith, participating in the work of God in history and identifying himself with God in Christ, as in Christ God has chosen to identify himself with man. The church

95

must build its program of worship and work on its certainty that such communion with God is man's high privilege and the source of man's life.

Second, its anthropology. The church's program of worship and work must take into account the biblical view of man as one who is created in the image of God for fellowship with the very God who created him, but who is completely unable of himself to enter into this fellowship, and unwilling to acknowledge his impotence and his dependence. The church must rest its program of worship and work upon its confession of its own sin, its identification with all sinful men, and its assurance of God's offer of new life.

Third, its ethics. The church must reflect in its worship and work the meaning of forgiveness and the nature of the new life made possible for man by God's gift of grace, and the obligation to bring the gospel to bear on the world's needs. The church must build its program of worship and work upon the fact that it is composed of forgiven men and that it has been entrusted with the stewardship of God's grace which is for all men who need forgiveness and a new way of life.

We come now to the church's conception of history. This chapter will attempt to show that in its worship and work the church must take into account the fact that God has spoken and that the Word of God is at work in history moving toward the fulfillment of his purpose for the world. The church is God's new creation, the present embodiment of God's activity in history. In itself it links together that which God has done and that which God will do.

Two tendencies in the church today lead us to this consideration of the meaning of history—namely, the church's tendency to picture the Kingdom of God statically and propositionally as though God were doing nothing and going nowhere; and the church's tendency to preserve itself as an institution whose end is its own being.

The doctrine of justification by faith implies a conception of history of great importance to the church. It is a conception of history which is found in the Bible and which explains the origin and nature of the church and establishes the purpose of the church. The Bible tells the story of God at work in history to create a people with whom he can live. It shows that the church is this people and is at the same time an instrument for creating this people. It shows that the Word of God is the dynamic of history operating in history from the beginning of time and continuing to work in history until the consummation of God's purpose for the world. The Bible declares its assurance of the outcome of history, its confidence that God's purpose of creating a family will be fulfilled in his good time.

The biblical story finds its climax in the life, death, and resurrection of Jesus Christ and the founding of the Christian church. As Nels Ferré put it in *Christianity and Society:*

> The New Testament is the result of an earthquake. When the Incarnation took place, which Whitehead in a personal conversation once called "the supreme moral moment of the world," a new basic reality and basic motif was introduced into history that played havoc with all previous ways of thinking.[1]

With these events there begins a new movement in the history of mankind. The creation is to be superseded and transformed by the New Creation of God, which is the church. The church is the heir of the Israel God once called into being. It is at the same time a foretaste of the Family he is to bring into being. It is the eternally contemporary body of those who dwell with God, and are learning by living with him how to be his.

The church rests on its past and is therefore a community of faith. It rests on its confidence that God has worked throughout history to bring man to the point where he can in some measure participate in God, and it rests on this story as living history which continues to come alive in the present whenever man accepts it as his story and enters into it.

The church looks to the future and is therefore a community of hope. It rests on its confidence that God will continue to work in history to bring to consummation his plan for a family in which all mankind may be gathered together about the feet of

God. It knows that what is done in the future will be done by God, as what has been done in the past has been God's. But it knows that it may participate in this story and serve as instrument for bringing about the consummation.

The church is a human community which, resting on the past and on the future, lives its life as all human beings do today and today only. It knows that what has been done and what will be done are God's. Only this moment can the church claim as its own, and this only because the church is God's instrument. But today with all its problems and needs is the responsibility laid upon the church by God, and only the church which exists today can tackle the job. This church we know with all its limitations and short-comings is God's agent in this present. It is because the church has been created by God and looks toward eternal life with God that the church has the courage and the wisdom to live today as the church.

FAITH'S INTERPRETATION OF HISTORY

The Nature of the Bible as Interpreted History

When we speak of the biblical concept of history, we are speaking not of literal history, but of interpreted history. The Bible contains the story of a people as they themselves were able to interpret it through their faith. The events recorded in the Bible are not recorded in just this way in the history of neighboring peoples. The Exodus, which was the birth of the Hebrew nation, caused no ripple on the pages of Egyptian history. The birth and life and death of Jesus Christ, which was the decisive moment of all history for the Christian church, was barely mentioned in Roman chronicles.

This does not mean that these events did not happen. There is as little reason to doubt their occurrence as there is to doubt the birth, life, and death of George Washington or William Shakespeare. It means that these events had for men of faith a spiritual significance far beyond their political consequences. Egypt and

Rome went on about their business. The establishment of a little family of people who knew themselves to be the people of God, the establishment of a little community who knew themselves to be the church, did not even make the headlines of the morning paper. But because faith was given the wisdom to grasp the significance of these moments, new movements in history were begun which were to affect the course of the world.

The story of Israel and of the Christian church found in the Bible is faith's interpretation of events. As Israel and the church took cognizance of these events in faith and went on living in the light of these events, the Bible record became for them the norm for life and the source of light. Holmes Rolston, editor in chief of the Board of Christian Education of the Presbyterian Church in the United States, has clarified this relation of Bible to history and to the church in a way that is particularly helpful.[2]

There were first of all, says Dr. Rolston, the revelation events —that is, events which occurred at a crisis in the life of the Hebrews and brought about a change of great moment. In the Old Testament this was the Exodus of the Hebrew people from Egypt and the establishment of an independent people. In the New Testament this was the Event of Jesus Christ—the longing of Israel for the Messiah, the birth, life, and death of Jesus Christ, and the founding of the Christian church. These were events in history which anyone might see and report.

The second step in the formation of the Old Testament was the people's recognition of the Exodus as an act of God to establish a covenant people, and in the New Testament it was the disciples' recognition of the identity of Jesus as the Christ of God. These were not facts of history reported by Egypt or by Rome. These were an interpretation of history by the people who were permitted by the Spirit of God to see the meaning of history. Their interpretation rested on the faith of the Israelites that God was at work in history, and in their own history, to fulfill his purpose for the world. It was this very faith that created first Israel and second the church, the New Israel, as the people of God.

The third step was the written record of this interpreted history.

The New Testament was written down as the church moved farther away from the revelation event, and felt a need for an authoritative statement of the church's recollection and interpretation of the event. The Old Testament was written in essentially the same way and for the same purpose. The written record, which was written by the church, thus became the only source of its knowledge of the Event to which it owed its existence as church, and thus to which it owed its faith. Then it became the norm for the church—the foundation of its proclamation, the description of its new life in Christ.

The Bible, then, which contains our only record of the events—or, if you prefer, of the Event—through which God has worked in man's life is interpreted history. It is history interpreted by faith. It is the record of the life of a people who conceived themselves to be God's peculiar people. It was written by this people themselves under the inspiration of the Holy Spirit, to interpret for themselves and for their children the meaning of these events which had brought them into being. It reflects their faith that the meaning of all history is found in their history, and that the meaning of their history is found outside of history. The fact that they framed their story in the largest possible dimensions of the Creation and the Consummation indicates the ultimate dimension of their faith. The God who brought the universe into existence, who controls its beginning and its end, is the God who has entered into their lives at significant points and has changed the course of their history through their response to him. The fact that they could see the incidents in their lives as the scene of God's work gave them a sense of the significance of history. It meant that for them no event in their lives could be interpreted as insignificant. The God who changed the course of their lives thereby changed the course of the world.

All people interpret history in one way or another, and the interpretation they give to history determines the meaning they attribute to life. The faith of the Hebrews that the eternal impinges upon the temporal at every point made it essential that Israel live its life in the light of the eternal. The faith that God has created the church to be the people of his Son Jesus Christ requires the church to accept the responsibility of paying heed to the Word of God, participating in God's plan and purpose in every phase of life.

Misunderstandings of the Nature of History

It will be easier to see the importance of the biblical understanding of history if we will take time to look at some of the alternatives to this view and what these alternative interpretations of history imply for their adherents. Four such views come immediately to mind. One of these is the classical Greek view; the other three are pensioners on the biblical view and may be thought of as Christian "heresies"—namely, the Humanist, the Marxist, and the Fundamentalist views of history.

To speak of the classical or Greek view of history at all is to speak without precision, for the Greeks had no real understanding of the significance and reality of history. Sociologists call their view the "cyclic" view of history. By this term they mean that events had for the Greeks no real meaning; they simply occur and recur again without purpose. For the Greek, meaning was to be found in the spirit world and man's spirit found meaning only when it could escape from history and enter wholly into the spirit world, of which this world is a pale shadow. Plato's figure of the cave comes at once to mind. One who holds this view may tolerate his daily life, but he will not take it seriously. It is illusory and man would do well to escape it.

The three views which follow may all be thought of as Christian heresies. All three depend on the seriousness with which the Bible interprets history, but they distort the Bible's interpretation. William Temple called attention to the fact that Communism is a Christian heresy. So also, it may be said, are Humanism and Fundamentalism.

The Humanist view and the Marxist view regard history as of the greatest significance; indeed, they think of history as itself the scene where reality may be found, and they regard history as having no reference beyond itself. The goal of history is realizable within history by a power which is itself located within history. The Humanist sees the dynamic of history within man, that is, in human knowledge and in human freedom. He contemplates a world in which a multiplication of scientific invention will bring an ever better way of life, disease will be wiped out, and life prolonged and made richer and fuller. As Reinhold Niebuhr puts it, this view regards "the historical development of man's power and freedom as the solution for every human perplexity and as the way of emancipation from every human evil. . . . Man not only creates the historical realm through his freedom, but he is himself subject to development through history because historical processes extend the power of his freedom indeterminately."[3]

One who holds to ideas of history based ultimately on the power of human freedom may exert himself strenuously to bring about the good society, but he will not set his sights as high as the biblical doctrine of man would allow, nor will he be as prepared for disillusionment as the fact of sin requires.

The Communist view of history differs from the Humanist largely in the nature of the dynamic of history which it perceives. Whereas for Humanism the dynamic is the human mind, for the Communist it is economic power. Man is at the mercy of an economic power in the universe which is working irresistibly to bring about community. In both Communism and Humanism there is a clear recognition of the significance of history and an inevitable movement toward a goal. In both this goal is seen in terms of community or the "good society." In both the movement and the meaning of history are self-contained.

Both of these pensioners on Christianity are weak in their conception of community, and both are weak in their understanding of the dynamic of history. But both are strong in their emphasis on the movement of history toward a goal and in the urgency which is aroused by their optimistic secular eschatology. As a matter of fact, the church must be continually on guard lest it give up to them its eschatological hope, ignoring its own revolutionary interpretation of history and turning it over to a heretical sect which threatens to use it to take the world from the Christ.

The Fundamentalist, though he claims to rest upon the Bible, is little nearer a biblical view of history than is either of the other Christian heresies. For the Fundamentalist misunderstands the nature of the Bible and thus simplifies and distorts it, and with it its view of history and its doctrine of God. The Fundamentalist separates biblical history from history outside the Bible as though the two were completely different phenomena. He secularizes all history outside the Bible as though God had nothing to do with it, and sanctifies all history inside the Bible as though God were the sole agent there, so that the continuity between the two is broken. Thus he is able to combine a very literal pseudobiblical eschatology with a thoroughly secular one without being aware of contradiction, and he comes out with a Hedonistic picture of heaven which disavows the very gospel itself, concerned with individual salvation without the need to participate in the sufferings of the world. The Fundamentalist fails to recognize that biblical history is history interpreted by faith rather than a record of uninterpreted events. Actually all history is the scene of God's action and all history is interpreted history. The historian selects and relates in accordance with a definite point of view. Biblical history is history interpreted by the faith of a particular people that God is at work in their lives to bring about the redemption of the world.

In reading the Bible as the literal history of events rather than as history interpreted by faith, the Fundamentalist foreshortens the hand of God and reduces the dimensions of life. A literalist is deprived of the use of symbols for expressing his faith in the reality of the ultimate dimension of life. He sees God in history as a figure of history rather than a figure of faith and thus reduces God to the stature of a giant man. The Fundamentalist refuses to recognize what the philosophers speak of as "second causes"; he portrays God as one who acts crassly and immediately in nature and human life. Seen in this dimension, God appears in the Bible story as arbitrary and unpredictable.

Instead of this, the Bible views history as the scene where the ultimate and the temporal meet. It portrays events of such significance and mystery that their meaning can be expressed only in symbols, which point beyond themselves to truth that man can trust but cannot fully comprehend. To the man of faith history becomes sacramental. It is "the bearer of the meaning of life," the scene where God enters into the life of man and man is enabled to enter into the life of God.

Each of these interpretations of history may be seen as misinterpretations of history. All of them fall short of the full meaning of history as it is interpreted in the Bible, and they lead to a misconception of the meaning of life. The Humanist is impelled to rise on his own freedom to ever new heights; but he finds that his freedom has led him to heights which he is unable to bear, and within which he only increases the tragedy and suffering of mankind. The Communist finds himself committed to anarchy and discord; he throws himself into strife believing that through strife peace can be found. But he finds that having taken up the sword he shall indeed perish by the sword. The Fundamentalist lives intimately with the God he sees at work in the Bible story, but in his literal interpretation of the story he destroys the ultimate dimension of man's life with God.

The Significance of the Biblical Account of History

The significance of the biblical account of history is that it presents in narrative form the simple faith of the church that God is active in history. In so doing it proclaims in the most vivid way possible the faith that God is a living reality in history, that by his Word he has brought into existence a living community, the church, which he claims as his own, and to which he has entrusted his purpose for the world.

The Bible is an account of the Living Word of God as he enters the history of man to win man into community with himself. It is the story of the Creation of the world and of the New Creation. At the point where God's own Spirit participates in the human spirit, and the human spirit begins to participate in the Spirit of God, a new movement of history begins. The movement of history is an irreversible process, in which each moment rests on the moment that went before and leads to the moment that comes after. Although the story begins beyond history, having its roots in the eternal, and the consummation is brought about beyond history, nevertheless the story is a real story that takes place in history where men live and make decisions. And the decisions men make when confronted by the Living Word are the wheels on which the story moves forward.

The amazing thing about the Bible is that it does not merely tell the story of the Word of God in human history. It actually *contains* the Living Word of God. The story stretches through time from beginning to end; nevertheless, the whole story—its beginning and its end and all its parts—is present to the man of faith in every moment of the story. The story is eternally contemporary. Like the church, it becomes a means for making the story move forward. The Word of God that spoke in the events still speaks in the events and catches up the reader into that which he reads. Thus the faith of the actor in the story and of the writer of the story is kindled afresh in the reader.

So real is this story, so true to the experiences of mankind, so sure the faith of the writers, that the reader finds himself drawn into the story as he reads. He identifies himself with the persons about whom the story is told. He is confronted by the God who takes the initiative throughout. So compelling is this sense of identification that even as I write I find myself unable to write impersonally of this experience and am driven to write of it as though it had happened to me. For as I read the Bible, the story of the Bible becomes my story.

It becomes my story in two different senses. In the first place it becomes my history as a member of the church. It is the story of the creation of this sacred community to which I belong. The Bible is our memory book, the inner history of the events which called us into being and gave us our life and our mission. It was because God spoke to Abraham, and Abraham left Chaldea and went to Canaan; it was because God called Moses back to Egypt to confront Pharaoh, and Moses responded in faith; it was be-

cause God came in Jesus Christ, and Peter gave up his fishing
nets to follow—it was because of all this that we belong to the
Christian church today and make the breath-taking claim to belong
to the body of Christ. These events are our history as members
of the church of Jesus Christ, as truly as George Washington and
Abraham Lincoln are our history as American citizens. The heritage of faith into which we were born was their gift to us.

Not only so, but the Bible story is my story in yet another way.
The Bible is no antiquarian book. It is a living story of a living
God. It is the spiritual history of a people in whose lives the
activity of God in all human history becomes visible. As I take
their story for the story of my past, I lay hold of their faith as an
interpretation of how God acts in my life today. I find myself
identified with the persons to whom he spoke then. His call to
Abraham becomes my vocation. I am a part of the people whom
God created. I too must get up with my family and my household goods and go into a land that he will show me. His rescue
of Israel from Egypt is a parable of my own rescue from bondage.
His covenant with Israel becomes his covenant with me. The
Bible is the mirror of the soul. It reflects all the profound experiences, the doubts, the sorrows, the triumphs of man. As I read
these stories, they become avenues through which God himself
comes to me, holding out new life, as he has always come to men
and women. They are the inner history of mankind, the spiritual
history of you and me. Through these stories I am made part of
the New Creation, the church.

THE BIBLICAL PORTRAYAL OF
THE CREATION OF COMMUNITY

The meaning of history is God's purpose to establish community of God with man. Thus the Bible, which tells of the
community, and the church, which is an expression of the community, are inextricably interwoven. In the story the meaning of
community becomes clear as nowhere else in human thought, and
the reading of the story helps to sustain the community it describes.

God's Creation of Man to Enter Into Community

From the very beginning of the story it is apparent that God's purpose in creating man has been that man may dwell with God. This, as we have seen, is the meaning of "the image of God." It is the significance of the face-to-faceness of God and man. Only when man is in the presence of God is his humanity a reality.

We find God's purpose for man symbolized in the garden as man walked with God. We find it symbolized again when the man and woman rebelled and hid themselves from God, and again when they were driven from his presence because of their rebellion. Then the real character of community between God and man begins to come clear, and the motif of the story, as God goes seeking man offering him covenant no matter what. For God is seeking to create community by offering community— which is the meaning of justification by faith and the significance of the church.

God's Invitation to Covenant

The covenant God makes with man sets the frame of community. Covenant is a guarantee of eternal fidelity, and an invitation to enter into fellowship on the basis of that assurance. The word "adoption," so important to Pauline thought, catches up all of this, as everyone who has ever adopted a child knows so well.

In Genesis and Exodus the lines which define community are sketched in. A man named Abram with nothing to offer but himself accepts God's invitation to be the father of God's people and a blessing to all the world. The Hebrew people, that were no people, were set free from cruel bondage and made a special people. The man and the people were given a hope, a destiny, a mission. They were given the assurance of God's love no matter what.

These are the marks of community as portrayed in the Bible: first, assurance of fidelity which is not contingent on anything the other person must do or be, but which rests simply on God; second, a power, a destiny, and a hope which are oriented beyond the community; third, a mission which includes all men everywhere, excluding no one. A community established along any other lines is unable to survive.

God's Own Presence in the Christ

The lines of community become firm in the Incarnation of God in Jesus Christ. Here community is established with the Twelve by means of a New Covenant of the heart. Peter comes to know the reality of grace in a person who forgives and forgives again, who takes upon himself the infidelity of Judas and in that act sets Barabbas free. The cost of community becomes clear—man's inability to keep covenant, God's willingness to pay. The historical manifestation of community is created in the church of Jesus Christ, the body of those who have identified themselves with the Lord of History.

With this there comes into being the New Creation of the people of God, the body of those who have been made new. But the church knows that the life of the church is not in itself but in God; that if God's purpose is to be accomplished in the world, it cannot be the church who does it. It can only be God. But it rests in the assurance that God's purpose will be done, and that because of God's love the church is to play a part. As a very recent writer puts it: "The Church is never more than the rebellious people of God, the sheep that have erred and strayed, the unfaithful bride, the body that absurdly wants to be the head."[4]

The Community Realized at the Great Consummation

The end of the story takes place beyond history, as the beginning does. The community God wills to establish is never the church; it is an eternal community of all men everywhere. The Kingdom of God is an eternal kingdom transcending time and place.

A. E. Taylor, in *The Faith of a Moralist*,[5] points out that when the word "eternal" is attributed to this community God will establish, the word "eternal" suggests a kingdom that can somehow gather up this whole movement of history into one great moment. The community to be established must be as real for one moment in time as for another. It must include Abraham and John Calvin as well as those who live at later moments of history. It must include those who live on the continent of Africa as well as those who live in Palestine. In this respect the community of the Communist, which is only for those who live at the end of the great Revolution, and the community of every Utopian dream, fail utterly. Unable or unwilling to recognize a reality beyond history, their very interpretation of history is truncated and their dream of community denied.

The end of history as men of faith have interpreted it is seen in terms of a community of men with God and with the heavenly hosts. "Then," wrote John, and the fact that he was exiled on a lonely island when he wrote shook his faith not one whit, "I saw a new heaven and a new earth; for the first heaven and the first earth had passed away, and the sea was no more. And I saw the holy city, new Jerusalem, coming down out of heaven from God, prepared as a bride adorned for her husband; and I heard a great voice from the throne saying, 'Behold, the dwelling of God is with men. He will dwell with them, and they shall be his people, and God himself will be with them . . .'

"And he who sat upon the throne said, 'Behold, I make all things new.' Also he said, 'Write this, for these words are trustworthy and true.' And he said to me, 'It is done! I am the Alpha and the Omega, the beginning and the end. To the thirsty I will give water without price from the fountain of the water of life. He who conquers shall have this heritage, and I will be his God and he shall be my son. . . .'

"And I saw no temple in the city, for its temple is the Lord God the Almighty and the Lamb."[6]

THE FUNCTION OF THE CHURCH IN HISTORY

The Church's Responsibility to Be Aware of God's Plan

Because of the unique place of the church in this story of God's work, the church has a responsibility that is given to no other.

The church must be aware of the plan for the world which God has revealed, and the church must let that plan inform its life in the world.

Too often the church has seen the work of God in Lilliputian terms. Its concept of salvation has been individual only. Its view of the Kingdom of God has been static. Its portrayal of the Christian life moralistic. Seldom has the literature of Christian education been informed by any adequate concept of eschatology, and as a result life under the Lordship of Christ has appeared spineless and unexciting.

The church must never lose sight of the bigness of God's plan. It must hold before its own eyes and the eyes of the world the meaning of history and the picture of the outcome to be anticipated. Only in the context of the total sweep of history can it understand the significance of its own life and the urgency of reconciliation with the neighbor. Only in this context can the church find the courage to face the tensions and complexities within its own soul and within the society of which it is a part.

The assurance that God is the Sovereign Ruler of history and that the outcome is in his hands; the assurance that his righteousness is writ deep in the structure of the universe where it controls and sustains and destroys; the conviction that even God's judgment is for man's salvation, and when responded to in repentance brings life; the conviction that God's whole energy of love is directed toward reconciliation and community—these are the meanings that are revealed to man through God's action in history, and that must permeate the literature of Christian education.

The church must proclaim its faith in God's saving grace as a revolutionary force in history. In this respect Communism, the heretic, is often truer to its task than the Christian faith from which Communism borrows its urgency. Communism proclaims the end in ringing tones and calls youth to the task. The fact that the church sees its goal beyond history rather than within history all too often causes the church to lose its urgency. The literalist who fixes a date on the calendar as the date of the end of history is not likely to forget the importance of the Day of the Lord, even though he conceives it in distorted terms. In losing the ultimate dimension which biblical eschatalogy provides he is likely to lose the dimension of triumph and grace, and of humility and sacrifice which the God of the Bible story requires.

The church has a concept of history that should send it out singing to adventure and sacrifice. It looks to a glorious consummation of the work of God in a fellowship of grace that gathers up all mankind who will come, and offers fulfillment in Christ Jesus. It offers an invincible Captain, whose name is Love. It makes no false claims to ease and luxury. Indeed, it promises humiliation and even a cross.

The church is prone in its educational program to offer Christ as a sweet-tempered friend, rather than as the Saviour of the world who marches to victory over sin and death. As such it offers one who makes no demands and offers no hope. And the world turns away in disgust, for it knows that such a Christ has no meaning for this world. An amazing thing about human beings is that the soul of man does not shrink from hardship when it catches a glimpse of the Suffering Servant as one who shares the hardship. Men and women who stay away from the church do so because it asks too little of them, not because it asks too much. Men and women want above all to give themselves to a cause bigger than they, to *spend* their lives for that which is most real and most relevant to human need.

The Christ of the New Testament is a prophet, a priest, and a king. He proclaims the truth about God's righteousness and love and calls man to a new kind of life with God. He enters into the presence of the Father as the very Lamb that was slain, taking on himself the burden of man's sin that man may be changed and drawn into community with God and man. He sets up in history so strong a reign of love that no man can experience it without being drawn to it or repelled by it. And the church is called to point to him who rules, and to point so clearly that no man may live out his days in ignorance of the fact that this is the meaning of life and this the destiny prepared for him.

The church's task is harder than that of the Communist, and

easier. It is harder because the church is compelled to acknowledge the tensions and ambiguities that arise from its awareness of the eternal dimension of life and to accept a responsibility for which it knows itself to be incompetent. It is easier because the church has been given the task by the Ruler of history himself and the outcome is as certain as the fact of God.

It is the burden of the church, and its glory, that it must acknowledge the tension inherent in its being the New Creation of God. A neat philosophy of history which packages up the gospel with index tabs on all its parts for easy reference will never do justice to the complexities of history which arise out of man's rebellion and God's grace.

No one can look at the church as it exists and believe that God means to use this to bring about a great eternal fellowship of all mankind. The church falls short at every point of being what it must be, and is. But if the church will in its teaching point beyond itself to God, whose church it is and in whose power it relies, the world can take heart that God rules and will rule. For the church is judged by the Word. Only when it is able to respond to God in repentance is it created afresh by the Spirit of God. As Reinhold Niebuhr points out, without the final eschatalogical emphasis which is found in the Bible, the church tends to equate itself with the Kingdom of God and thus threatens to destroy itself and with it the world.

The Church's Responsibility to Carry Out Its Mission

The church has three ways of carrying out its mission as the family of Christ and the instrument of the New Age. It must tell the Bible story; it must bear witness in its own life; it must be concerned for the world in which it is placed. Actually this is only one way and not three, for if any one of the three is missing, none of the three is valid.

In the first place, the church must keep continually before its people the Bible story. It must gather up and conserve in its life and worship this story of what God has done for man in the past and continues to do today, for this story is the story of its life and hope.

The church must tell this story and listen as it tells it, making the very telling of the story the means of remaining true to its Lord and of drawing the world to him. It must bring the revelation events into the present, where the meeting of God and man may take place again. Then may the church be judged and re-created by the living Word and sent out again on its mission.

Too often the church has lost this dramatic movement of the Bible story in the fragmentary and moralistic use of the Bible in its teaching program, and has as a consequence painted the Christian life in somber colors. We have let people think Christ came into the world simply to tell children to share their toys and to tell adults not to smoke or play cards; we have failed to tell them that he came as a part of God's eternal plan to draw all men into community with God.

The church must organize its educational program in such a way that the Bible is open for its members, in order that individuals as well as congregations may be continually confronted by the Word of God. The Bible is the only source through which the people of God may be kept aware of their heritage and brought into meeting with the Word as he has moved in history. Only here can we know the Incarnate One in his incarnation, and identify ourselves with the New Testament church which was brought into being by its life with him. It is not enough for the minister to proclaim the Word from his pulpit—although this he must do—nor is it enough to have eloquent teachers lecture on the Bible. The Book must be opened to the people in such a way that they may themselves enter into the story and meet God in the events of redemption where God speaks most clearly of his forgiving love.

Thus the church is under obligation to give all possible help to its people in order that they may know how to read the Bible. It is no easy thing to read a story written two thousand years ago in such a way that the event of the story becomes alive again. There is need for an understanding of the nature of the book as interpreted history, and for principles of interpretation by which the meaning may be made clear. The church has too often lacked the faith to be honest about the nature of this treasure. It has feared that its members would be unable to cope with the complexities of a living revelation which comes in earthen vessels. But the treasure must come to earthy man in earthen vessels. The faith of the church is that it can retain the treasure even so, since it is the Word of God which comes.

Moreover, the church must weave into its very life and worship its living memory of what God has done. In everything it does it must preserve these events, entering into them as eternally contemporary. It must read the Bible story as the story of God's call to the church today to enter into covenant with him. It must know its sacraments as a recollection and a re-enactment of God's work for man and man's response to God.

Baptism, which is man's identification with Christ's dying and rising again, becomes a means of entering covenant with God at the price of God's Son. Although occurring only once in a lifetime, it is a perpetual sacrament, guaranteeing our inheritance until we gain possession of it.

The Supper, which is repeated again and again throughout the life of the Christian, is a perpetual reminder of God's sacrifice for man's affection and loyalty, and a means of continual renewal for all "those who wish to have Jesus for their life."[7]

The Apostles' Creed is a narration of the whole Bible story of Creation, Incarnation, Redemption, which every time we repeat it brings alive our dependence on God's works of love.

The Christian Year is a drama cycle in which the story is told again and again in festival and song, in repentance and mourning, in surrender and re-creation—the Advent, the Passion, the Resurrection, Pentecost. Through its very acts of worship the church must catch man up and identify him with the whole stream of God's work for man's salvation.

The church must conserve and interpret its past in its own worship, because it is a living past in which the church finds the source of its life, the dynamic for the present, and the hope of its future. It must give attention to the sacraments and to these sacred occasions so that its people may be aware from childhood that these observances are windows into another dimension of life, links that bind this world to that eternal world which impinges upon the temporal at every point. We have been too matter-of-fact about our religion—mundane and this-worldly. We have been pedestrian and unimaginative. It is almost as though we have feared to suggest anything in our educational program that we could not see through to the end, as though we had chosen to close windows to the souls of boys and girls lest the mysteries of the ineffable God should take them where we fear to lead. Our educational program must do everything it can to lift the heart of men to the undreamed possibilities God holds before them in his Son Christ Jesus, and to the unquestioned power made available to us in his Spirit.

In the second place, the church must offer its own life as the context of nurture in the faith. It has been said before in these chapters that the church not only has a story to tell; it must also offer itself—its worship, its work—as the context of nurture, drawing the world into the church where God has promised to meet man.

As a person is drawn into the church to participate in the life and worship of a congregation of the people of God, he may find himself involved in living encounter with God himself, who is worshiped here as Creator and Redeemer and Lord. Here as the church confesses that it has strayed from God's ways like lost sheep and prays for his mercy and restoration, as it ascribes praise to God for the majesty of his creation and the beauty of his holiness, as it calls upon him for his blessing upon those he has claimed for his own, the meaning of life with God becomes clear.

The church has too often assumed that it could perform its task of nurturing its people in the faith merely by establishing formal classes where it can talk about the faith, and it has assumed that the Sunday school is the seat of its major educational endeavor. Faith defined as deep trust in God, which is required by the doctrine of justification by faith, is far more than an intellectual understanding of and acquiescence in the creeds of the church, and can be fostered in persons only by inclusion in the community of faith. This community of the covenant people of God, where God's action for man's salvation becomes contemporary in every generation, serves as matrix in which men and women and boys and girls can be brought to know the truth that all history is under the rule of God and can be drawn into the stream of God's redemptive work for the world.

This requires that the church think of the curriculum of Christian education as a congregational curriculum, in which the worship and work of the congregation becomes the context and means of nurture, and the school of the church assumes its proper place as the agency in which understanding of the Christian heritage of faith can be passed on. The church must recognize that the Christian faith involves participation in covenant with God and man, and that only a self-conscious covenant community can communicate such a faith by drawing persons into a living covenant relationship.

This does not lessen the importance of the Sunday school. It defines its function more precisely and makes it far more significant than before, for it supports the work of the Sunday school by providing through other channels of the church's life the reality which may be the object of study in the church's school. Study of the Bible, of the history and heritage of the church, of the obligation of life under the Lordship of Christ, becomes meaningful now because the student—child, or adult—has already come to know the God who speaks through the Bible and the church, calling to life under the Lordship of Christ. As he lives in a Christian family, as he observes Christian citizens and businessmen, as he participates in corporate worship, and enters into the church's mission, an individual is led to know beyond the shadow of a doubt that there is an eternal that impinges upon the temporal and that those who have entered into covenant with the Eternal God have found the way to life. Then may individuals have the courage to put their faith in God and enter with confidence into life with him.

Life with God means a miracle of new birth to those to whom the church is able to communicate the Word. It means reconciliation and community in a world where lines are drawn tight and barriers lifted higher than our banners. It means courageous men and women who are not afraid of what men say of them because of the love of Christ. When this is so, when the church is faithful to its Lord, the Word of God, which speaks through the story of God's action in history, will speak also through the life of the church, which is his body.

In the third place, the church must remember that the Word of God speaks with clarity and urgency in every generation in terms of the needs of the world to which the Word comes. The church will be guilty of passing down an irrelevant heritage from the past, the memory of a Word which spoke in the past but speaks no more, unless the church will listen to the Word of God with its eye on its own condition and will make provision within its own program of study and work for a careful analysis of the world in which it lives and the relevance of the Word in that world.

The Word of God is a living Word, sharper than a two-edged sword. It comes in judgment upon the church and upon the world, and only when man responds to judgment in repentance does it bring redemption. The church may not dare to listen to God's Word or to encourage its people to listen without expecting to be rebuked and chastened. For the church has identified itself with the world rather than with God and is guilty of sin as the world is guilty. So the church must acknowledge its own involvement in the sin of the world before it goes out to battle against it.

But the church must proclaim to its people also God's forgiveness on condition of repentance and God's call to be Christ's family in the world. It must put into its educational program all possible provisions for study of the meaning of this call in the situations in which its members stand. It must in its fellowship give courage in the face of conflict, and continual assurance that the battle is the Lord's and the outcome is in his hands. It must in its preaching and teaching proclaim to its people the responsibility to enter into the battle as the instrument of God's revelation of himself and the steward of his reconciling and forgiving grace.

The church has been content with a church-centered program which puts emphasis on maintaining the institution at the expense of its mission. The tendency in our church school has been to stress attendance—even to the point of giving awards for unbroken records, and of setting up competition between classes—although the church is the body of One who was willing to give up his own life for the sake of the world. To establish a program of works —whether the "works" be attendance at Sunday school or filling out blanks in a workbook—is, as Paul told the Galatians, to follow another gospel which is no gospel at all.

The church's educational program must always point beyond the church to the Christ as the Source of life and to the world as the recipient of it, teaching its people that they are the agent created by God through Christ's death and resurrection to serve as his witness and his instrument in this generation; that Christ's movement in history requires them as his people; that companionship with him in his work is the condition of life. It must set the task of studying seriously the world in which God has placed us in order that the community God wills to establish throughout the world and throughout all time may be established here and now where the church's only responsibility lies.

The doctrine of the Incarnation is our clue to the fact that service of God is best expressed in service to man, that identification with God in covenant is identification with One who in the Incarnation identified himself with every man who has ever lived and calls us to the same identification. God "presents himself to us in our brothers," said Calvin, "and in their persons demands from us what we owe him."[8]

CONCLUSION

The church in every age is called to be the bearer of the Word of God to its own age. Its mission as the people of God is that the

Word may live in the world transforming the world, as the Word lived in Christ two thousand years ago.

The dimensions of the mission are such that the church draws back in dismay, aware that what it is called to do it cannot do. Throughout the centuries it has devised many ways of covering up its impotence. Today it depends on most of those same ways of covering up. It intellectualizes its faith. It re-defines sin and new life in little, manageable terms. It presses for goodness rather than for love. It ignores its eschatalogical hope. It pretends a piety it does not know. It does these things to relieve the pressure of God's call it has heard in Jesus Christ.

But the church is called to be the people of God, and the terms of the call are God's terms and not man's. The church's role is to listen and to respond, to accept the offer of covenant and the promise of fidelity no matter what, to undertake his mission in the confidence of his sovereignty.

For the church is the point at which God comes to man in tenderness and love, in judgment and forgiveness, in power and victory. And the church is the point at which man may come to God in repentance and hope. The church is under the compulsion of God's love to accept its dual role—striving to express in its life and work what God would say to man, relying on his forgiving and victorious love to overcome its failure and to renew its hope.

References

Chapter One: Words Without Knowledge and the Living Word

1. For this discussion of the changing views of revelation I am drawing heavily upon John Baillie's *The Idea of Revelation in Recent Thought*, New York: Columbia University Press, 1956.
2. John Calvin, *Commentaries*, p. 232. (Volume XXIII, *The Library of Christian Classics*). Newly translated and edited by Joseph Haroutunian in collaboration with Louise Pettibone Smith. Philadelphia: The Westminster Press, 1958.
3. John Calvin, *Institutes of the Christian Religion*, III, IV.
4. From "Choruses from 'The Rock'" in *Collected Poems 1909-1935* by T. S. Eliot, copyright, 1936, by Harcourt, Brace & World, Inc.
5. Calvin, *Commentaries*, p. 228.
6. Emil Brunner, *The Divine Imperative*, p. 76. Philadelphia: The Westminster Press, 1947.
7. *The Heidelberg Catechism in German, Latin, and English*, p. 153. New York: Charles Scribner's Sons, 1863.
8. Galatians 2:20.

Chapter Two: No Easy Sainthood

1. David Roberts, *The Grandeur and Misery of Man*, p. 186. New York: The Oxford University Press, 1955.
2. For this treatment of the oneness of man, I am indebted to Balmer Kelly, who presented this point of view in an unpublished lecture in Montreat, North Carolina, in the summer of 1958.
3. John 17:21.
4. E. LaB. Cherbonnier, *Hardness of Heart*, ch. 5. (Christian Faith Series, Reinhold Niebuhr, Consulting Editor), Garden City, New York: Doubleday & Company, 1955.
5. *Ibid.*, ch. 8.
6. Calvin, *Commentaries*, pp. 230-231.
7. Dietrich Bonhoeffer, *Ethics* (Ed. Eberhard Bethge), p. 151. New York: The Macmillan Company, 1955.
8. Brunner, *The Divine Imperative*, p. 72.
9. Cherbonnier, *op. cit.*, p. 127.
10. Calvin, *Institutes of the Christian Religion*, III, III, 1 and 2.
11. Bonhoeffer, *op. cit.*, p. 94.

CHAPTER THREE: We Are All Barabbas

1. Pär Lagerkvist, *Barabbas* (Tr. Alan Blair). New York: Random House, Inc., 1951.
2. Hosea 11:8-9.
3. Romans 6:5.
4. Calvin, *Institutes of the Christian Religion*, III, III.
5. Calvin, *Commentaries*, p. 327.
6. *Ibid.*
7. James D. Smart, *The Teaching Ministry of the Church*, p. 161. Philadelphia: The Westminster Press, 1954.
8. Calvin, *Commentaries*, p. 327.
9. Fedor Mikhailovitch Dostoevski, *The Grand Inquisitor*, p. 20. New York: The Association Press, 1948. (Translated by Constance Garnett.)
10. Cherbonnier, *Hardness of Heart*, p. 62.
11. Joseph Sittler, *The Structure of Christian Ethics*, pp. 72-73. Baton Rouge, Louisiana: Louisiana State University Press, 1958.
12. *Ibid.*, p. 73.
13. Alexander Miller, *The Renewal of Man*, p. 88. (Christian Faith Series, Reinhold Niebuhr, Consulting Editor). Garden City, New York: Doubleday & Company, 1955.
14. *Ibid.*, p. 90.
15. Paul Ramsey, *Basic Christian Ethics*, p. 89. New York: Charles Scribner's Sons, 1951.
16. Miller, *op. cit.*, p. 44.

CHAPTER FOUR: The New Creation

1. Nels F. S. Ferré, *Christianity and Society*, p. 95. New York: Harper & Brothers, 1950.
2. This point of view about the Bible is set forth in a paper entitled, "The Nature of the Bible, and Its Interpretation and Use in the Educational Work of the Church," prepared in connection with the Curriculum Improvement Program of the Board of Christian Education of the Presbyterian Church in the United States.
3. Reinhold Niebuhr, *Faith and History*, p. 15. New York: Charles Scribner's Sons, 1949.
4. Werner Pelz, *Irreligious Reflections on the Christian Church*, p. 13. Naperville, Ill.: SCM Book Club, 1959.
5. A. E. Taylor, *The Faith of a Moralist*, Vol. I, Ch. III. London: Macmillan and Company, 1930.
6. Revelation 21:1-3, 5-7, 22.
7. Calvin, *Genevan Confession*.
8. Calvin, *Commentaries*, p. 326.

Index of Authors and Subjects